Brolga Country

Brolga Country

TRAVELS IN WILD AUSTRALIA

Mitch Reardon

JACANA BOOKS

ALLEN&UNWIN

First published in Australia and New Zealand in 2007

Jacana Books, an imprint of
Allen & Unwin
83 Alexander Street
Crows Nest NSW 2065
Australia
Phone: (61 2) 8425 0100
Fax: (61 2) 9906 2218
Email: info@allenandunwin.com
Web: www.allenandunwin.com

National Library of Australia
Cataloguing-in-Publication entry:

Reardon, Mitch.
    Brolga country : travels in wild Australia.

    Bibliography.
    Includes index.
    ISBN 978 1 74114 991 3.

    1. Brolga - Australia. 2. Brolga - Habitat - Conservation -
    Australia. 3. Wetland conservation - Australia. I. Title.

598.30994

Design by Seymour Designs
Maps by Map Graphics, Brisbane
Index by Trevor Matthews
Printed in China by Imago

10 9 8 7 6 5 4 3 2 1

PAGE I: *Brolgas in misty silhouette herald the beginning of the day with rolling clarion calls as they cross an Atherton Tableland winter skyline.*

PAGE II: *A preening brolga nibbles the base of a feather and then draws it through the bill so that the little barbs reconnect, much like a zip fastener. Brolgas spend much time caring for their feathers but the feathers still wear out. The main flight feathers are gradually replaced during a postbreeding moult when the birds experience a short flightless period.*

OPPOSITE: *Pearly morning light shines through the mist that blankets egrets, pelicans and whistling ducks poised on the banks of a tropical billabong.*

PAGES VI–VII: *Rosy twilight fills the sky as brolgas return to their roost at Bromfield Swamp.*

For my grandchildren, Alex and Sophie, in the hope that the wild places that gave me so much pleasure while researching this book will still be thriving when they grow up

Contents

Acknowledgments

Except for the far north Queensland leg of my odyssey, when I had the companionship of my old bush mate Steve Nott, I travelled through brolga country alone. But the solitude was frequently broken by wildlife enthusiasts and others who provided friendship and their knowledge for no other reason than their own generosity. For kindness, advice, assistance and incidental hospitality I am especially indebted to Claire Harding, John, Lynne and Nick Anderson, Emily Tyson, Steven Bourne, Jack and Pat Bourne, Brian Robins, Terence Reardon, Jason Ritchie, Fran Davies, Jan O'Sullivan, Arthur Palmer, Brian Stone, Duncan and Alex Robertson, Peter and Kate Waddell, Gwyneth Nevard, Craig Mills, Julia Deleyev, Stephen Garnett, Laura Phipps, Ali Ben Kahn, Mike Schultz, Keith Hutton, Mike Helman, Suzanne Coates, Mick Smith, Jarrah MacGregor, Carol Hall, Geordie and Faye Williams, Jane Rowe and Julian Reid.

I would also like very much to thank Matthew Herring, Rebecca Sheldon, Elinor Scambler, Mark Stoneman, Tim Nevard and Frank Badman, who were good enough to inspect the finished manuscript for any errors and distortions. They are, of course, in no way responsible for any errors that may remain. And finally, I am most grateful to my editors, Louise Egerton and Angela Handley, for their guidance and encouragement.

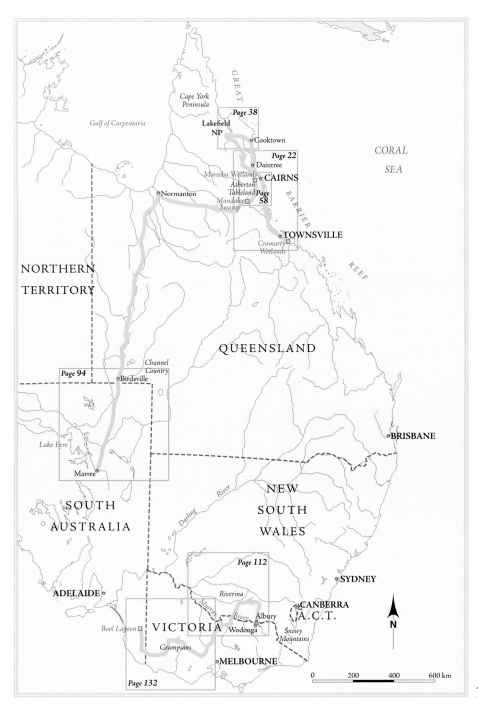

The author's journey.

Introduction

An incubating brolga parent settles gently down on the pair's eggs. Generally just two eggs are laid each year and usually only one dominant hatchling survives. This low reproductive rate slows recovery from population losses.

PAGES X–1: *A dawn patrol of busily feeding waterbirds freckles Clancy's Lagoon in the Mareeba Wetlands.*

In the winter of 2004 I set out on the first of what would become a series of outback journeys to observe and document brolgas in their natural habitat. Fuelled by curiosity and a sense of adventure, I embarked on an unhurried and richly rewarding odyssey that perfectly complemented my lifelong attraction to wild country. Everything I could wish for was contained in the stillness of Australia's big ancient landmass. Despite the rigours of hard travel, my quest to learn as much as I could about that elegant creature, the brolga, invariably induced in me a glad-to-be-alive exhilaration.

The only member of the world's fifteen crane species endemic to the Australian region, brolgas were called the native companion in colonial times because they were said to accompany Aboriginal people on their wanderings. To some, however, they will always be known simply as those tall, leggy birds that dance.

Brolgas seemingly engage in their highly stylised 'dance' for any reason, at any time, although it's used principally as the showpiece in their elaborate courtship rituals. Displays are initiated by young unpaired males in search of mates or when bonds are renewed between established pairs. Standing opposite each other, wings half-open and shaking, they advance and retreat, bowing and bobbing their heads. High jumps are interspersed with sudden stops, when an amorous bird will throw back its head and trumpet a loud, wild love song. Often the excitement spreads through a group, until the whole flock is leaping and pirouetting like an enchanted ballet troupe.

My travels to see at first hand the brolga's mysterious ways ultimately took me to some of northern, eastern and southern Australia's most beguiling and important wildlife habitats. Like a bird on a migration binge, I looped across great swathes of the brolga's range, visiting fabled destinations from far north

Covered in grey down and weighing only 100 grams, a newly hatched brolga chick's first growth occurs in its long legs. As soon as it is strong enough to keep up, it is led away from the increasingly conspicuous nest into the sheltering marsh.

Queensland's steamy coastal wetlands and lushly textured tropical rainforests to the wilderness of Cape York Peninsula's Lakefield National Park. From there my months-long journey of discovery took me through Mareeba Wetlands to the beautiful Atherton Tableland in Queensland's high country, one of the northern brolga's most important dry season flocking sites. I then headed west to the home of the desert brolga, where it's easy to mistake the bareness for barrenness. But patience revealed that life has a good hold in this harsh terrain. In the more temperate and developed southern states, I learnt that the local brolgas are in danger of extinction due largely to the conversion of wild land into farmland. Help is on the way, though, and not a moment too soon. My travels ended at sublime Bool Lagoon, the last great gathering place for brolgas in the south-east.

Well before I reached my final destination, I began to find that my brolga odyssey was turning out to be much more significant than I had anticipated. It dawned on me that in many ways this regal bird's beauty and vulnerability are a poignant metaphor for our vanishing wild places. The brolga's ability to survive in Australia's changing landscapes broadly reflects the successes, failures, aspirations and problems of the country's wildlife estate as a whole. Successfully conserving brolgas, I came to realise, means keeping entire ecosystems functioning in good working order.

Leaping and flapping their spread wings, a majestic pair of mated adult brolgas reinforce their bond with an elaborate and enthusiastic courtship dance. Comprising intricate sequences of coordinated bows, theatrical jumps, runs and short flights, dancing is the most spectacular of all the brolga's social behaviours.

Brolgas are what ecologists call an umbrella (or flagship) species, the protection of which shelters and conserves other animals and plants. Researchers now know that the condition of birds like brolgas, who live at the top of a wetland's food chain, is a sensitive indicator of their aquatic habitat's overall health. By paying attention to celebrity species like brolgas, ecologists and land managers also attend to the survival needs of the natural systems that support them. Since brolgas require clean water and air, these icons of the wild give us a clear lens through which we can view environmental trends.

With habitat loss and degradation such a chronic threat, the secret to the brolga's survival is habitat, habitat, habitat. They won't survive without ample wetlands. That's also true of many other species. Migrating waders use wetlands like stepping-stones on their journey, flying from feeding ground to feeding ground, so a disturbance at one could be catastrophic. People also need wetlands as filters for groundwater and nurseries for fauna and flora.

We prefer to think that we're different from other animals but at a cellular level we are fundamentally the same. Yet somehow we've forgotten that we belong to the natural world. In every corner of the globe people seem at odds with their life support systems—cutting them down, squaring them off, draining them of species and flexibility. But people and wildlife ultimately draw their food and water from the same source. We won't survive if other species don't. Technology will allow humans to adapt to diminished or degraded resources for longer than most other animals but not forever. In that sense, this book is as much about Australia's most precious commodity—water—and the brolga's fellow creatures, including humans, as it is about brolgas.

These ideas engaged me on my travels through brolga country. Out there I could, every day, so it seemed, learn something new from something old. But the privilege of being able to sink into the solitude of nature will never be ours solely because we wish it.

Encouragingly, there are increasing signs that the message is getting through. Southern brolgas—whose future rests largely in the hands of individual landowners—have inspired a broad coalition to help protect them from further habitat loss. Farmers are beginning to realise that the wellbeing of the cranes is a portent for the future of the farmer. Enlightened policy makers are demonstrating at last the kind of natural resource management the 21st century cries out for. From places that still ring with the brolga's wild and wonderful bugle comes a clear, constant refrain: saving nature in all its splendid variety is the only way to go if we plan on going the distance.

Competent land stewardship recognises the simplest truth: the land that produces our necessities must be preserved.

CHAPTER ONE

Cromarty Wetlands

Now they are standing close together
Others are flying from Mamururi
Up there circling Ngiwalkirri
Kurruwurwur!
Now they are standing close together.

Others are flying
Closely approaching
Others are following from Karangarri
They are remembering
Now they are telling
Others are flying from Karangarri.

—TRADITIONAL ABORIGINAL SONG-POEM¹

According to the Ancestors, in the Tjukirita time when the Earth was flat as a disc, there lived a beautiful young woman named Brolga, renowned as a dancer of wondrous skill and grace. Brolga knew the old dances—parading like an emu, whirling like the wind—and invented new ones that told tales of wild beasts and ancestral spirits. Admirers came from afar to see her dance; the more she danced the more famous she became.

Early one morning Brolga left her gunyah and went to the nearby plains to dance in the shade of a favoured old coolabah tree. As tiny puffs of dust rose from her feet, the malevolent spirit Waiwera descended from a black hole in the Milky Way, saw Brolga and determined to possess her. Quickly he spun himself into a whirlwind called a willy-willy and swept her away.

Brolga's people became worried when she didn't return. 'Maybe another clan has stolen her from us.' 'No, we would have heard her cries.' Recalling her favourite place, they went to the old coolabah tree. Brolga's tracks had been blown away but they were able to follow the trail left by the willy-willy.

Many days passed until finally the searchers caught up with Waiwera and their beloved Brolga. Without hesitation all the men rushed to the rescue, brandishing spears and boomerangs. Realising he could not escape with Brolga, Waiwera made sure no one else would have her, then fled back to his home in the Milky Way.

At first it appeared as if Brolga had vanished, too, until a child cried out: 'Look! There's a bird that we've never seen before!' A beautiful, tall grey bird slowly stretched its wings and instead of flying away it began to dance. It thrilled the watching people with the same abandonment and poetry of motion that Brolga had displayed. The bird came closer and then the people understood. Unable to take Brolga's elegance and love of dancing with him, Waiwera had changed her into a bird that to this day everyone calls the brolga.

Brolga's transformation could have happened here, where I stood gazing at the Cromarty Wetlands. The big birds inhabit fresh and saline wetlands, grasslands and cultivated areas from Shark Bay in Western Australia to south-eastern South Australia, and this narrow zone of dry tropical north Queensland coastline, 40 kilometres south-east of Townsville, seemed the perfect setting to nurture new life.

PAGES 8–9: *A family group of brolgas—long necks outstretched and immense wings beating the air with a distinctive rhythm—crosses Cromarty Wetlands in unhurried flight.*

OPPOSITE (top): *In laboured but strong flight, a skein of magpie geese heads for fresh feeding grounds. Of all Cromarty Wetland's many waterbirds, the magpie geese and brolgas seem the most finely attuned to life in the wet–dry tropics..*

OPPOSITE (bottom): *Taxiing for take-off. Spray flies as a plumed whistling duck runs as hard as it can across a pond's smooth surface while furiously flapping its wings to generate lift.*

I gazed about me at saltpans decorated at the margins by palm-like pandanus and fringed by mangroves. To the east freshwater swamps, covered almost entirely by dense swards of bulkuru sedge, are separated from the tidal influences of coastal streams to the north and south by marine plains lush with salt-tolerant grasses and herbs. Lily-filigreed lagoons extend into backwaters sheltered by paperbarks.

These marshlands are bracketed on their landward side by the steep forested slopes of mounts Elliot and Burrumbush—granite ranges formed 280 million years ago by buckling and volcanic upheavals when Australia was at the leading edge of a moving continental plate. On their seaward flank, the swamps and lagoons merge with the Haughton River and estuary before flowing into the Bowling Green Bay wetland system and finally debouching into the Coral Sea. Over everything lies an immortal tropical light, like transparent silver.

I visited Cromarty shortly after sunrise one fine July morning. My guide was Mark Stoneman, a bluff, articulate beef rancher and ex-Queensland government minister who, in middle age, is still robust and full of vim. 'What's unique about Cromarty Wetlands is the range of attaching land and marine systems—creeks, woodlands, rainforest, fresh and saline swamps, a river and estuary—all contained within 40 kilometres from the top of that mountain watershed to the Great Barrier Reef,' he enthused. 'I doubt such varied and concise connectivity occurs anywhere else in the world!'

Clearly, Mark is enraptured by this protean ecosystem and though his knowledge was invaluable to me, it was his contagious enthusiasm bubbling forth that captured my imagination. As he explained his ideas and hopes, it struck me that here was a conservationist for our times: one who recognises that if we are to save what remains of our wildlife, idealism simply isn't enough. There have been too many noble failures. To tackle the vexed question of sound land stewardship, Mark advocates a rational approach, where the human economy is in practical harmony with the nature of the place and the entire community, natural and human, is present in it.

Earlier we had stopped to open a padlocked gate that gave us access to the core wetland, contained within a cattle property and closed to the public. We then drove slowly along a narrow track, stopping frequently so I could focus my camera or binoculars on scenes of bountiful birdlife.

Parties of brolgas walked around very sociably, ankle-deep in water, using their purpose-built stabbing bill to dig tuberous bulkuru sedges (or spike rushes) from the mud. Flocks of magpie geese crowded deeper waterways; their irregular half-musical honks filled the air. Every so often a long-legged goose would upend or submerge its head in the water to excavate bulkuru tubers from the swamp's muddy bed with the hooked tip of its short, powerful beak.

Starchy, high-energy bulkuru (*Eleocharis dulcis*) root tubers (or water chestnuts) grow in huge quantities in Australia's tropical aquatic pastures—one site studied averaged 5 million of these fleshy perennial freshwater bulbs per hectare. They are the food of choice for brolgas and magpie geese, and a favourite with traditional Aboriginal people. Brolgas are omnivorous,

Male and female brolgas look alike. Their imperious yellow eyes are enclosed by naked orange to bright-red skin, except for small grey ear tufts—all that remain of this bald-faced bird's ancestral feathered head. The bare red skin engorges during courtship displays or battles for dominance, making it even brighter in colour.

As water levels in Cromarty Wetlands begin to decline from early July onwards, magpie geese congregate in shallow swamps to feed on broken-down bulkuru sedge that has flowered and seeded. The geese harvest the bulkuru tubers by upending and digging for them in the watery mud with their robust hooked bill.

selecting the seeds and corms of aquatic plants, insects, spiders, molluscs, frogs, small reptiles and, nowadays, the introduced house mouse. But so critical to the northern brolga's diet is this one plant that the annual cycles of the bird and the sedge are intimately interwoven. And though both brolgas and geese subsist on bulkuru, each species has its own harvesting technique and ecological niche, thus ensuring that direct competition for the resource is kept to a minimum.

Brolgas flying from one feeding ground to the next passed close by overhead—I could hear their throaty '*corop, corop*' contact calls and the rush of air over slow-stroking, up-flicking 2-metre wingspans that propelled them along at 70 kilometres per hour. A flotilla of pelicans— looking, in the near distance, like plastic toys—glided above the far shore of a broad channel that abuts Mount Elliot. Waders on long stilt-like legs were either standing in the shallows or walking in a stately manner, one clawed foot raised, held, then solemnly lowered, in a parade along the waterline. Now and then, black-winged stilts uttered small wintry cries and everywhere the waterways were punctuated by the sharp white outlines of egrets and spoonbills.

A resident of Cromarty's open forests and woodlands, this forest kingfisher waits motionless on a bare branch before launching a superbly controlled dive in pursuit of a beetle, bug, spider, grass-hopper, worm, frog or small reptile.

It was exhilarating to be in contact with this watery landscape so elemental to true nature. Its thronging waterfowl continually reinvented the scenery. Yet for all its ecological diversity and despite being part of one of the most extensive waterbird habitats in Australia, Cromarty is still not Ramsar[2] listed. Unlike neighbouring Bowling Green Bay, a Ramsar-listed national park, Cromarty Wetlands falls mainly within a series of freehold properties. The non-profit Wetlands and Grasslands Foundation, of which Mark Stoneman is a director, has an option to buy the entire core property and intends to seek Ramsar listing once the sale eventuates.

Much of Mark's energy is currently devoted to furthering the cause of wildlife conservation on private land. About 5 per cent of Queensland is national parks, 10 per cent is urban dwelling, roads and other public lands, and 85 per cent is privately managed, he tells me. 'Government is constantly pressured to create new havens for wildlife but funding is limited. When land is acquired it means an increased demand on park management funds.'

Because most northern brolgas are highly mobile—responding to seasonal rains by flying long distances to nesting sites—they are difficult to conserve solely in protected areas. Though no sanctuaries have been specifically established for them, Queensland national parks such as Staaten River, Mitchell and Alice Rivers, and Lakefield, protect wet- and dry-season habitat and support resident breeding populations. However, most prime brolga habitat in Queensland is on private or Crown land, including critical coastal wetland breeding sites around the Gulf of Carpentaria and western Cape York Peninsula. Mark's foundation aims to further conserve brolgas, their habitat and associated fauna and flora by expanding the private sector's role.

Until recently, northern brolgas survived by keeping out of harm's way. Their security relied on the unsuitability of their remote breeding grounds for disruptive farming practices. But in north-east Queensland's large coastal wetlands in particular, increasing agricultural demand has led to disturbance and loss of foraging habitat. Fewer brolgas are now seen at traditional east-coast dry season sites, reductions that in some places exceed 50 per cent.

Cromarty Wetlands' first real exposure to development came in the mid-1970s when much of the adjacent Burdekin River delta's best alluvial land was converted into sugar cane and rice plantations. The rice soon attracted the attention of hungry brolgas and magpie geese, which in turn attracted the ire of growers. Both bird species are protected throughout Australia but in Queensland a Permit to Take may be issued if it can be demonstrated that a protected species is causing damage to crops. A regrettably high tally of brolgas and geese were shot and poisoned before rice-growing was deemed unprofitable and farmers switched to sugar production, now the region's main crop. These days, brolgas feeding in Cromarty's southern marshes do so against a backdrop of the local sugar mill's belching smokestacks.

Though signs of encroaching industry are unsightly, as long as brolgas are not actively persecuted they can adapt remarkably well to some forms of human land use. Cranes and people have coexisted successfully for generations in rural areas around the world. On occasion cranes have even benefited from humankind's progress. The brolga's taste for fallen grain prompted a population expansion in the Northern Territory, the Kimberley and other parts of Western Australia, when cereal crops were developed there from the 1920s, and those brolga populations continue to increase.

Looking back on my stay at Cromarty Wetlands, the first stopover on my travels, I now realise that portents abounded, although I didn't recognise them at the time. This little-known sanctuary turned out to be a perfect microcosm of the modern brolga's ever-evolving world. Like wetlands all over Australia, Cromarty is under great stress from expanding human population growth and industrial development. At the same time, however, a small band of nature's guardians, down to their last options, hurry to achieve workable and ethical environmental protection strategies before it's too late.

TOP: *Cromarty's brolgas have adapted to life in the shadow of a sugar mill but ecologically fragile ecosystems such as wetlands are limited in the kinds of development they can sustain. Well-managed wetlands provide for the needs of humans, while also allowing room for brolgas and other wildlife to flourish.*

BOTTOM: *Mark Stoneman, director of the Wetlands and Grasslands Foundation.*

CHAPTER TWO

Townsville to Daintree

Brolga was out walking when she saw Emu with her many chicks. Jealous Brolga hid her only chick and said to Emu, 'What a weary life, feeding so many babies! Take my advice and kill them before they tire you to death.' Foolish Emu listened to the soft words and destroyed all her children. After her cruel trick, Brolga twisted her neck so quickly to call her chick that she strangled her pretty voice and was left with only a harsh, discordant cry.

—'WHY BROLGA HAS A HARSH VOICE', ABORIGINAL CREATION STORY

From Cromarty, I planned to drive north to Townsville and then to the regional capital of Cairns on a road that starts as a sinew of asphalt then dwindles to gravel as it pushes through tropical lowland rainforest following the Pacific coastline to Cooktown, the most northerly hamlet on Australia's east coast. Beyond Cooktown my route would become a corrugated dry-weather track sketched in the sandy orange earth. This single access road passes through a far-flung wild frontier that is, to this day, a byword for remoteness. It also supports brolga habitat as priceless as any in Australia.

Several years earlier I had overlanded to the tip of Cape York Peninsula, drawn by an impulse to experience Australia's iconic adventure safari. This time I was going only as far as Lakefield National Park, but the prospect of even this curtailed expedition was enough to excite my imagination and I departed Cromarty with the quiet thrill I always feel at the beginning of a long journey.

My first stop was nearby Townsville Town Common. As its name suggests, this 3300-hectare remnant of the once extensive Bohle River Basin wetlands originally served as a community paddock for livestock brought to the Townsville market. It was also home to huge aggregations of waterbirds during the wet and post-wet seasons. From January to August, flocks of brolgas and honking magpie geese flying in wedge formations between the common and the Cromarty–Clevedon wetlands were a feature of the Townsville skyline. To ensure the protection of these feathered legions, the Common was proclaimed a conservation park in the late 1970s.

A series of walking tracks and marked trails has been established to provide visitor access to the park's mangrove-fringed tidal estuaries, woodlands, grasslands, vine thickets and swamps. Shouldering camera bag, tripod and binoculars, I set off along the Forest Walk that follows the edge of a billabong set about with paperbarks, eucalypts and acacias.

My approach alerted a pair of Radjah shelducks. They froze in the water, poised tense and motionless with upstretched necks, then took off in a panicky whirr of wings, complaining loudly and leaving behind a gentle ripple. Gazing out of soft and watchful eyes, a small mob of agile wallabies

PAGES 18–19: *The quiet sanctuary of Townsville Town Common draws a squadron of brolgas as monsoon clouds roll darkly off the Coral Sea.*

OPPOSITE: *In Daintree's lush and humid rainforest, elegant Alexandra palms can grow 30 metres tall as they strive for maximum exposure to the sun.*

BELOW: *A rainbow lorikeet laps nectar and pollen from a copiously flowering silk cotton tree,* Bombax ceiba. *Townsville is the silk cotton tree's southern limit—the deep red blooms welcome dry-season visitors from the southern states to Queensland's tropical far north.*

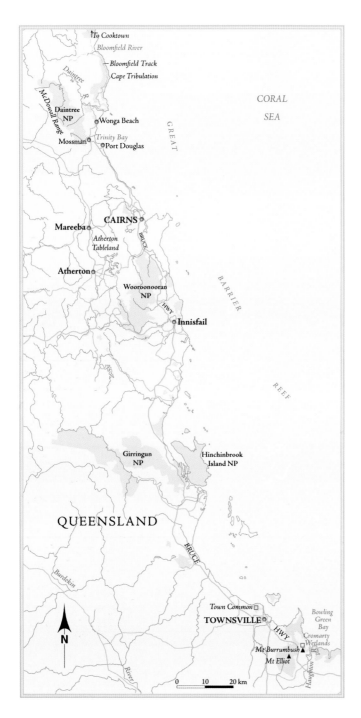

propped to watch me pass before bounding away with startling speed, swerving and dodging with the erratic leaps that earned them their name. A rainbow bee-eater in pursuit of a wasp darted low, flashing glints of electric green; its prey grasped firmly in its bill, the bee-eater returned to its perch with a glittering display of the coppery iridescent sheen beneath its wings. Overhead, a handsome Brahminy kite rode the morning breeze, languidly circling in a featureless sky.

Before leaving home I had seen photographs taken in former times of thousands of brolgas gathered in the park's lagoons during the post-wet phase when water and food were abundant. During the day I spent exploring the park I saw only two. Their absence is due largely to a plague of invasive exotic plant species, which in various combinations nationwide has left entire ecosystems in disarray.

In the Townsville Town Common Conservation Park weed invaders include rubber vine, noogoora burr, chiney apple, lantana, stinking passionfruit and snake weed. But the most problematic are guinea grass (*Panicum maximum*) and para grass (*Urochloa mutica*), which ran rampant following the well-intentioned banishment of cattle after the common was declared a park.

Overgrazing and trampling by cattle has severely degraded too many wetlands in northern Australia, resulting in the progressive loss of their original water plants together with their rich communities of aquatic insects, crustaceans, frogs, freshwater turtles, native fish, and small native mammals such as water rats and swamp rats. Deprived of vegetation to feed on or rest in, water-birds, including brolgas, soon depart degraded wetlands.

At first glance, excluding livestock from wetlands would seem to make sense but the reality is more subtle than that.

There is evidence that controlled grazing can do more good than harm where wildlife such as brolgas is concerned. Totally excluding cattle promotes rank growth around wetlands, which may force brolgas to desert their roosts. At the Townsville Town Common it wasn't long before the ungrazed marshes became choked with para grass, a hardy, aquatic perennial with 4-metre long tendrils that established mattresses with a biomass of up to 20 tonnes per hectare. Meadows of valuable bulkuru sedge were overwhelmed, severely impacting the birds reliant on them.

Brolgas and magpie geese all but disappeared. The rare clamorous reed-warbler's feeding grounds were also imperilled, as was the habitat of birds migrating from Asia and those migrating north–south within Australia. Researchers realised something needed to be done. A joint partnership project between the Queensland Parks and Wildlife Service, CSIRO, Burdekin Dry Tropics Board and community volunteer groups is currently exploring how various combinations of grazing and fire can best be used to reduce guinea and para grass and bring back native plants and wildlife to the common.

Properly used, cattle can be an essential tool of judicious habitat management. It's all a question of how and when. When to reduce stock numbers, when to apply pressure to a particular pasture, when to allow regeneration, how best to control or remove pests—in other words, how to balance the productivity of a complex and fragile piece of the planet.

Trailing two long white tail plumes, the buff-breasted paradise kingfisher flits about the Daintree's green and shadowy depths like a big buff-and-blue butterfly. Each year in early November these spectacular kingfishers fly from central New Guinea to their breeding grounds in tropical north Queensland's coastal rainforests and depart again the following March.

Pressed against a tree trunk, the rainforest-dwelling leaf-tailed gecko's wonderfully cryptic green and brown pigments and mottled skin pattern render it virtually invisible. This Gondwanan relict's camouflage is further enhanced by a broad flat tail and irregular outline, which eliminates even the smallest shadow. If a predator grabs the gecko's fatty tail, the gecko is able to detach it by reflex muscular contraction and escape.

The pros and cons of grazing wetlands highlights the delicate balancing act demanded of pasture and wildlife managers. The task of managing the remarkable variety of ecological complexities that characterise our natural world must satisfy a range of seemingly conflicting goals. Environmental management is a new science and inexact. Managers have no textbook to consult to learn the consequences or propriety of tinkering with nature's patterns and functions. Even the best-intentioned plans can fall prey to the law of unintended consequences. What managers do know is that while the old laissez-faire approach of 'let nature take care of her own' might satisfy an idealised view, it's unhelpful when attempting to protect biodiversity. We've come too far for that luxury.

I was thinking about the conundrums confronting wetland managers as I drove the 350 kilometres to Cairns, where I stopped to take on supplies, renew old acquaintances and meet up with Stephen Nott, an Aussie friend from my Africa years. Steve had flown up from Sydney to join me on the tropical Queensland segment of my brolga expedition. Once our chores were done, we headed north on the Captain Cook Highway in a burst of breezy sunlight and high anticipation.

Hugging the Pacific shoreline, we passed turquoise-blue, millpond-smooth Trinity Bay, named by James Cook on Trinity Sunday in June 1776. The scenery on this 60-kilometre stretch to the resort village of Port Douglas is downright dramatic—a visual feast of golden beaches, jungle-clad headlands and mysterious dark islands. On our left, to the west, the bulky spine of the Great Dividing Range rose in ridges and shoals of mist, its rainforest flanks crossed by plashing streams. In places the mountain wall plunged directly into the ocean. A green radiance seemed to lift off the crest of the mountains into the dome of blue porcelain sky, then disappear in swirls of feathery clouds travelling dreamily westward.

These stands of old-growth forest have been saved by the rugged topography but beyond, en route to the sugar milling centre of Mossman, the preponderance of clear-cuts and sugar cane is disheartening. Since the time of the first European settlers, 85 per cent of Queensland's ancient lowland

Black-necked stork parents both take part in nest building, egg incubation and the feeding of young. Although they look alike, yellow eyes distinguish the female from her black-eyed partner. At this age the uncomely brown and white chicks are often left on their own while their parents fill up on fish that they later regurgitate for their ravenous chicks. On hot days the parents transport water the same way to cool the chicks.

With its spiked armour and dewlap, the 60-centimetre Boyd's forest dragon is reminiscent of creatures from the age of reptiles. In its rainforest home in Queensland's wet tropics, this master of disguise blends so well with its surroundings that forest dragons were once thought to be rare. However, recent research has shown that in suitable habitat they can be quite common.

OPPOSITE: *Two pugnacious agile wallabies square off in Townsville Town Common. These young males use their powerful forearms to grapple in a playful wrestling bout that will help establish dominance.*

rainforests and 75 per cent of its upland rainforests have been victims of a chainsaw massacre and an axe massacre before that. Cedar-getters were already active in the Mossman area by 1875, when a small group of settlers planted maize, rice and coffee. Citrus-growing and bee-keeping also helped them survive until the sugar boom of the 1880s.

The new conquerors embarked on a Promethean mission to hack up this wilderness and build a world that belonged to them, a world that fitted their particular vision. On the one hand, theirs is a story of pioneering heroism, but they also left a legacy that can only be described as desecration. In the span of one man's lifetime, pristine forests were converted into farmland and sixteen distinct groups of Indigenous rainforest dwellers were dispossessed from homelands occupied by their ancestors for a thousand genera-tions. Clear-felling continued into the 1960s and 1970s. 'It was just ball and chain, slash and burn,' one logger conceded in retrospect. 'It all had to come out and what didn't come out we'd bulldoze and burn.'

Such an alarming magnitude of habitat degrada-tion, fragmentation and loss has had profound implications for rainforest biodiversity, to say nothing of the loss of photosynthetic activity, which plays a vital ecological role in balancing water, oxygen and carbon dioxide in the Earth's atmosphere. And though cleared rainforests may be fertile for a time due to the practice of unlocking the nutrient value of felled vegetation by burning, the dry soil soon deteriorates. Erosion becomes an immediate problem as the forest canopy no longer protects the loose, friable red basalt

soil from torrential downpours. The thin surface layer of organic material is rapidly lost, its nutrients leached away. Expensive chemical fertilisers are substituted, continuing the long-term exhaustion of the soil, but nothing can prevent sediment and nutrient run-off. Environmental considerations aside, there is also the cost to Queensland's economy, especially the con-tinuing damage to the adjacent Great Barrier Reef, which is worth far more in terms of tourism than the agriculture being extracted.

The manicured rows of sugar cane had given way to more natural vegetation by the time we reached the Cape Tribulation turn-off. A few kilometres on, we arrived at the cable ferry that shuttles vehicles across the grey-green Daintree River, its waters sliding slowly

away past dark forested banks. On the northern shore lay the eternally green Daintree River valley, set down behind mountains and hemmed in by the vastness of the Pacific Ocean.

In 1988, some 894,420 hectares of Queensland's wet tropical rainforest were inscribed on the UNESCO World Heritage list, with a provision for a total ban on commercial logging. The Wet Tropics World Heritage Area contains 733 separate parcels of land, including national parks such as Daintree, Barron Gorge and Wooroonooran; state forest; other public land; and about 2 per cent that remains privately owned.

The 17,000-hectare Cape Tribulation section of Daintree National Park extends in a narrow, discontinuous strip from the Daintree River in the south to the Bloomfield River in the north, with steep McDowall Range on its western perimeter. This is the Australia of the humid tropics—walls of dense, succulent, saturated greenery, lush, riotously overgrown, endlessly germinating—part of the oldest surviving rainforest on the planet.

Although I could find no archival records of their presence, brolgas very likely once existed even here in this almost impenetrable jungle, wherever low-lying, waterlogged areas gave rise to extensive wetlands. Depressions caused by impeded drainage in the topography appear from the air as regularly spaced holes in the canopy of dark green trees. Brolgas would have used these more permanent waters to feed and roost in during the dry season after ephemeral wetlands on the western hinterlands' floodplains had evaporated. It's a tradition still preserved on a small scale by brolgas that visit remnant wetlands in highland rainforests.

Shortly before crossing the Daintree River, Steve and I visited a sugar plantation near Wonga Beach, where Canadian wildlife artist Fran Davies is rehabilitating an old sugar cane paddock. Already this natural catchment is assuming the characteristics of the paperbark and acacia wetland it once was. Helped by an $11,000 Heritage Trust grant, Fran is also busy re-establishing the original swamp forest and hopes to reconnect it to the southern arm of the Daintree River.

'Eight months after the project started there were brown-backed

OPPOSITE: *As dusk approaches, a rufous night heron preens itself before flying from its daytime tree shelter to forage alone along the Daintree River's shallows and shoreline. Both sexes of this handsome watch-and-wait hunter have two or three permanent fine white neck plumes that are raised as part of their courtship display.*

honeyeaters nesting in the paperbarks overhanging the water,' she recounted with quiet pride. Many other bird species reappeared after the habitat began to recover. 'My biggest coup was a rare painted snipe that made herself at home.' Rainbow fish and emperor gudgeons arrived, 'although I don't know where they came from. Perhaps their fertilised eggs were carried in on the feet of wading birds.' Whether brolgas ever return remains to be seen but in former days they would have been seasonal visitors to these forest marshes.

Although brolgas are now virtually absent from the Daintree and other animal and plant species are threatened by past practices, this tangled world of sunshine, rain and warmth represents the largest block of tropical rainforest in Australia and retains its richest fauna diversity. It was like a time capsule that allowed me to see what these lowland rainforests looked like before Europeans intervened.

Queensland's wet tropical rainforests make up only 0.01 per cent of Australia's area but they support one-third of its marsupial species, one-quarter of the frogs and reptiles, 58 per cent of its bat and butterfly species, 20 per cent of its bird and 65 per cent of its fern species. This astonishing biological diversity includes almost 30 rainforest communities as well as around 700 plant and 85 vertebrate species that exist nowhere else in the world.

To get a sense of the teeming life in the Daintree's 200 million-year-old forests I needed to walk them, although other than the main road and several self-guided boardwalks most of the park is inaccessible except to well-equipped bushwalkers. Nevertheless,

once camp was pitched, I set out to tentatively pick my way through the smothering undergrowth, following a creek to avoid getting lost.

More than anything else in these tropic climes, I was struck by the light. From morning's earliest moments the sun ignites into a blowtorch of brightness but on entering the forest's mossy shade I had the sensation of crossing a threshold. There was an immediate change in climate—the crepuscular jungle gloom felt cool and damp. The transition was so abrupt it was almost like diving from a boat into the sea, as though the closed canopy was the surface and I was far below on the ocean bottom.

The sheer enormity of the luxuriant growth rising from the soil was almost overpowering. The trees, the light and the scale are all different to those of younger forests. I looked around and saw a catacomb of columns—monumental trees towering 30 metres— Daintree hickory, North Queensland rosewood, Noah's walnut and Alexandra palms. Their trunks carried a cargo of climbers and were decorated with epiphytic mosses, lichens, orchids and ferns. Woody liana vines, some as thick as an athlete's thigh, draped to the ground. Many trees have massive supporting buttresses spanning out from their trunks because the soil is so lacking in nutrients that the roots find nothing if they go deep. Strip away the rainforest and you're left with barren ground—the wealth is up in the treetops.

It's the lack of nutrients in the soil, many researchers believe, that accounts for the rainforest's diversity. To prosper in their crowded universe, plants need to grow quickly and unceasingly, employing ever more inventive

A dazzling beach north of Cape Tribulation is pounded by breakers churned up by a storm front while crested terns battle the wind. 'Here began all our troubles,' lamented James Cook after the Endeavour *was holed near here, although the native Kuuku Yalanji people knew this place more benignly as Kurranji, meaning 'cassowary'.*

A male Australian brush-turkey in Daintree National Park descends from a communal tree roost at daybreak to begin scratching on the forest floor for his breakfast of insects, fruit and seeds. Australia's biologically exciting tropical rainforests are filled with primitive plants and fauna that have evolved from ancient Gondwanan stock.

strategies to hoard nutrients, catch water, pollinate and go to seed. In the absence of sufficient space on the ground, plants will sprout in the canopy and send roots to the forest floor. All this competition means trees stand a better chance of surviving among trees of different species, because an insect or virus attacking one tree won't so readily affect others of the same species.

The uppermost storeys of the trees were dappled with glistening spots of light. A few bright shards dropped further down but in most places the forest floor was without any direct sunlight. This dynamic green cosmos is powered by sunlight but only a little more than 1 per cent reaches the forest floor. Some plants survive on just a few minutes of dappled light per day.

Butterflies fluttered by like erratic beams of light, specimens with wings

like white brushstrokes on blue stained glass, vermilion wings and green wings that turn purple when rotated in the light. A gorgeous metallic blue and black Ulysses butterfly bounced along with the curious flight pattern of a wind-up toy. From the high canopy came the songs of unseen birds; the whipcrack call-and-answer of a pair of eastern whipbirds, a paradise riflebird's harsh shriek, the loud ringing chatter of Lewin's honeyeater and the distinctive booming baritone *wallock-a-woo* of a wompoo fruit-dove.

This closed, claustrophobic world is so different to the surrounding habitat that the forest walls act like the bars of a cage, keeping the animals of the rainforest confined. I was reaching the periphery of that world; the ocean was nearby and I felt its breath booming against the edge of the continent.

It was already late afternoon when I stepped back into the sun-dazed zone—a dazzling space of beach sand, with gulls screaming overhead. I'd arrived at the edge of the galvanised seam where two landscapes crash into each other, where the rainforest meets the reef. It's a magic place, this fringe, combining the two worlds. The blue of the sea lightly covers the coral below. The water's silky surface was intermittently ruffled and shirred by schooling fish. A cormorant dived, disappeared, resurfaced, a fingerling in its beak. A flock of crested terns flew down the shoreline, their white undersides flashing like fine confetti as they banked.

For a long while I sat quietly, relishing the immense solitude. It was deeply contenting sitting there with the weight and distance of the continent behind me, sitting on the edge of existence. Out over the water a white-bellied sea eagle soared on broad, upswept wings, looking for fish. Shrill cries ricocheted across the forest crown—a bachelor party of king parrots whizzing home before dark. The sun was setting over the deep green forest and the deep blue of the wild horizon briefly flared king-parrot scarlet. To the east, where night had fallen over the Coral Sea, a three-quarter moon rode in a clear void of black sky. Before sunrise the next morning, Steve and I would break camp and then follow the narrow, winding Bloomfield Track as it climbed steeply through mountains and dense rainforest en route to Cooktown and the wild brolga country beyond.

CHAPTER THREE

Lakefield National Park

A very long time ago [the brolga] found a ground chilli and not knowing what it was, ate it, with the result that not only did his head take on a scarlet colour, but he got all hot and 'all same drunk'; it was during this predicament that he learnt his [dance] steps.

—ABORIGINAL CREATION STORY, W.E. ROTH, *THE QUEENSLAND ABORIGINES*, 1898

Steve and I headed out of Cooktown driving north-west on a route blazed in the 1870s by prospectors rushing the Palmer River goldfields in the unexplored interior. On this bright still day of winter, serenaded by a yellow oriole's bubbling song, under a dome of blue sky neither troubled by the scream of jets nor punctured by pylons there seemed little to complain of.

I like going outback. It suits my taste for remoteness and solitude, and helps rekindle a link, in style at least, to my younger vagabond days. Out in the bush I can give myself over to the palliative of the simple life. Emancipated from irksome obligations and material excess, I am once again master of my own destiny. And Steve Nott is the kind of companion to have on a trip like this.

Though neither of us had approached via Cooktown before, Steve had visited the peninsula in 1986 while single-handedly circumnavigating Australia on horseback—a four-year, 18,000-kilometre feat of skill and endurance that the prestigious Royal Geographical Society acknowledged by awarding him a fellowship. Only someone as at ease in the bush as Steve is could have done it. Like many bushmen, he's physically tough yet easygoing, low-key and unpretentious by nature. Sturdy and angular and bristling with beard, he's happiest in moleskins and khakis, with a sweat-marbled Akubra perched almost permanently on his shaggy head.

Around 40 kilometres from Cooktown we took a sharp turn west onto a lightly travelled road that, 5 kilometres further on, crosses a small creek downstream from miniature Isabella Falls. We drove in silence, each assessing the big wild unknown prospect ahead. Much of the country between Cooktown and the Tip, as Cape York is known locally, is without human presence—a 207,000-square-kilometre triangle of rainforests, wetlands, alluvial floodplains and woodlands cut by serpentine rivers that branch out like giant arteries with capillary-like tributaries. The few towns, such as Laura and Coen—fuel stops on the way to the Tip—are rough-and-ready frontier-style settlements, where a single long look usually reveals all there is to see. With a population of less than 20,000, Cape York Peninsula

PAGES 34–5: *Like weathered tombstones, wedge-shaped magnetic termite mounds—all aligned in a north–south direction to deflect the midday sun—dominate Lakefield National Park's grassy Nifold Plain.*

OPPOSITE: *In northern Lakefield, a mated pair of sarus cranes occupies their preferred habitat—a small wetland in open woodland.*

Skipping between delicate water snowflake flowers, a comb-crested jacana father hurries his chicks out of harm's way. For baby jacanas, managing their disproportionately long and awkward legs and toes on the tilting and sliding waterlily leaves takes some getting used to.

is one of those few places where natural wonders still take pre-eminence over human use.

The rutted dirt track we were following worked westward, plunging upward through montane forest flanking rugged Battle Camp Range, part of the northerly tending axis of high ranges and plateaus that form the Great Dividing Range's most northerly section. Months later, in Victoria, I would traverse its most southerly section.[1]

Beyond the crest, the ground fell away to reveal a landscape of unanticipated grandeur. Below, the Laura Basin's broad floodplains extended into Lakefield National Park. The shape of the crocodile-full Normanby River running down from the west lay in a pale serpentine of mist between fringing gallery forest.

The new country presented itself simply, in exciting white light. Dominated by tropical eucalypt and paperbark woodlands interspersed by grasslands, these floodplains support a huge wetland system made up of deep waterholes in the main rivers, oxbow lakes and back swamps, which fill when it floods to form an integrated drainage system.

As I peered down at this mighty panorama seemingly untouched by the smallest sign of human life, pale glints beside a distant marsh caught my eye, revealing themselves through binoculars to be a pair of brolgas. Motionless and mute, as if lost in thought, they stood transfixed in the vastness of those wide Australian spaces.

It was mid-July now and deep into the dry season. As pools recede during the winter drought, enormous post-breeding assemblies of waterbirds—cranes, cormorants, spoonbills, ibises, jacanas, ducks, geese, egrets and herons—gather at permanent waterholes, lakes and lagoons. Congregations like these are one of Australia's most dazzling wildlife spectacles, although this year unseasonally late rains had recharged ephemeral wetlands and delayed the birds' build-up.

For at least seven months of each year the region sees very little precipitation. Then, in the short December to March peak wet season, monsoons, troughs, tropical cyclones and south-easterly air streams deposit more than 90 per cent of the annual rainfall. The sky sags with humidity as bulging clouds drawn in by the scorching summer's back draft roll off the South Pacific and disgorge over 1000 millimetres of driving rain. Raging torrents cascade off the Great Dividing Range's steep escarpments and into the park's river network.

Trees fringing the Normanby River serve as a daytime camp for hanging clusters of little red flying foxes. As the sun sets, these rusty brown fruit bats (right) begin to stir. Day ends and the sky fills with their silently flapping shapes (below) as they set forth to harvest nectar and pollen from the blossoms of arid-adapted eucalypts and paperbarks. Little reds are the most nomadic of all flying foxes and important pollinators and distributors of seeds.

A mated pair of brolgas struts rhythmically through sedge beds bordering a marsh near Kalpowar Crossing. Well-established brolga pairs remain together for many years, staying near one another most of the time and synchronising activities such as feeding and resting.

The Normanby, Bizant, Morehead, Laura and North Kennedy rivers burst their banks to become a broad and burly flood, sandy brown and swollen with silt, that spreads out across the plains, transforming them into one vast wetland mosaic. Roads are impassable as whole savannas become lakes. Ultimately this watery world drains north past tide-flooded mudbanks and leathery green mangrove shorelines into Princess Charlotte Bay.

The rains stir wetlands to a vibrant new flush in their annual cycle. Until the wet season the brolgas have stayed together around the last water sources, but as storms become more frequent and the breeding season approaches, hormone-fuelled males become increasingly aggressive and anti-social. Young that remained with parents through the Dry are driven off and join up with other non-breeding brolgas to live in small outcast flocks. Bonded pairs have dispersed to their nesting territories by late February when flooding has subsided and swamps and lagoons are full, although heavy downpours still occur and early nesters risk having their nests drowned.

These immense breeding swamps now come alive with the egg-filled nests of thousands of waterbirds, including a sizeable but as yet uncounted complement of brolgas. Most of Lakefield's waterbirds breed at this time, when it's so lush you can almost hear the vegetation growing and food is superabundant.

Defined by its seasons, this is a land unto itself, both old and ageless, a vision from a time beyond memory but still persisting. As we drove deeper into the park I could imagine myself back in an age before European settlement, for despite its wonders Lakefield remains relatively unknown and retains the feel of undiscovered country.

By late that afternoon we had set up camp at 12 Mile Waterhole on the lower Normanby River in the New Laura section of the park. The campsite was sunlit and lovely, a place of golden mornings and silvery afternoons shot through with birdsong.

In the starlit pre-dawn, the maniacal racketing of blue-winged kookaburras ushered in the new day. Sunrises as orange as a scrubfowl's foot marked the changeover from the kookaburras' cacophony to the pheasant

TOP: *This yellow-speckled, three-month-old red-tailed black-cockatoo fledgling will soon depart its nesting hollow high in a Lakefield eucalypt. Till then, the lone chick waits at the entrance in the mornings and evenings to be fed.*

ABOVE: *Steve Nott map-reading at beautiful Breeza Lagoon.*

coucal's tremulous melody, like a cascade of pure water. Big, slow-moving mobs of red-tailed black cockatoos, their funereal plumage set off by brightly coloured tail bands, trumpeted brassy contact calls as they crossed the sky. Those silver-tongued songsters, pied butcherbirds and olive-backed orioles, delighted with their mellifluous clear notes. The somnolent crooning of peaceful doves and diamond doves soothed throughout the day, but of all the diurnal bird sounds, the predominant voice and the one I associate most with these sunstruck tropical woodlands was the melodious, high-pitched *coolicoo* of the bar-shouldered dove.

Warm windless evenings provided their own brand of native night music. The eerie wails of bush thick-knees; the woebegone howls of a dingo, alone under the big night sky; the resonant and incessant *chof-chof-chof* of a large-tailed nightjar; and the deep, pulsating exchanges between a pair of Papuan frogmouths that haunted the paperbarks lining the river.

The male frogmouth was particularly trusting of campers; in my spotlight, his red eyes floated in the dark like hot coals. One unusually warm evening our gas lantern encouraged an invasion of moths and other winged things, including black crickets, which quickly caught the male frogmouth's attention. He flew from branch to branch, assessing the situation, then launched a low pass to snatch his first cricket. The hunting was so good that before long he ignored us and concentrated on the chase. One inspired swoop set the fixated frogmouth on a collision course with Steve, averted at the last moment when he pulled out of his dive with an open-mouthed shriek of alarm.

One of the first things I did after setting up camp was check the banks of the large perennial waterhole we overlooked. I was scanning for signs of crocodiles, especially the well-used haul-outs where they bask on winter days and the chutes down which they slide into the water if disturbed. Growing up to 6 metres long, the primitive-looking saltwater (or estuarine) crocodile is the world's biggest surviving reptile and an occasional predator of people. Our waterhole was deep, scoured out by floods during successive wet seasons—a time when subordinate male salties seeking fresh territory venture far upstream from the coast. As the Dry advances and rivers evaporate, some big crocs get marooned in the deeper pools. Staring at the latte-coloured water I couldn't help wondering if somewhere beneath the surface nightmares lurked.

A croc lying in wait for me to come and collect water would use its powerful tail to propel itself out of the pool and up the bank to snatch me the same way it

OPPOSITE: *An old male saltwater crocodile suns itself on a riverbank. Its stony eyes glint with a savage watchfulness, intense and predatory. Huge jaws, pitted and corroded like chunks of cast iron and studded with long sharp teeth, are one of nature's most efficiently designed traps. Salties are the world's largest surviving reptiles and occasionally seize unwary humans.*

RIGHT: *Eerie nocturnal whistles and wails rising in pitch are often the only sign that a bush stone-curlew (or bush thick-knee) is about. By day the stone-curlew stands still to avoid detection, relying on its patterning for camouflage in its grassed, open-woodland habitat.*

would a wallaby. A ranger I spoke to at Lakefield headquarters pointed to a steel cage he'd recently used to capture a 'problem' croc—'a 16-footer with half a foot of tail missing,' he drawled laconically—that had been taking dogs from an Aboriginal outstation at nearby Kalpowar Crossing.

'Crocodiles literally swarm in these waters,' reported Walter E. Roth, Northern Protector of Queensland Aborigines, who in 1898 carried out the earliest anthropological research in the district.

The natives here have but little dread of these creatures … Where necessity demands that a known crocodile-infested river has to be crossed, and there is no canoe, the black manages it by diving, a method which I had an opportunity of witnessing on the Lower Normanby River. Gliding silently below the surface of the water, he keeps close to the bottom; if it is too wide, he loses no time in coming up for a breath of fresh air and down again; should he come across one of the saurians, he immediately stirs up around him the dark mud on the river bed, and makes good his escape very much on the same lines as a cuttlefish when in danger.

Flicking its long forked tongue in and out of its mouth, this 1.6-metre-long sand goanna detects scents by 'tasting' the air. A forked tongue is common to all snakes but the goanna is the only lizard to possess one. Like snakes, goannas also have a Jacobson's sensory organ in the roof of the mouth, which analyses the sensations the tongue picks up. These two features help the goanna to follow trails left by its prey and perhaps to find a mate.

A year after our visit, a regular tourist to Lakefield was fishing from a canoe in the Normanby when he was attacked by a 4-metre saltie. He tried to fend it off with his paddle but to no avail. With one thrash of its heavy tail, the crocodile suddenly surged upwards and grabbed the man's arm in its arsenal of rough jutting teeth. Then the water closed behind them leaving only viscous brown bubbles.

Barry Jefferies vanished without a trace, although his wife managed to swim to safety. Two large crocs were later trapped; the second one caught was believed to be the culprit although officials concede they can never be certain. All the signs indicated our waterhole was croc-free but I remained alert when collecting water. You can never be too careful where salties are concerned.

Life in all its dangerous, complicated, annoying glory teemed in this sun-tilted paradise. To some, it might look like the end of nowhere but that's

A female bustard nervously flares her wings. Standing about a metre tall, with a 2.3-metre wingspan, this mighty species shares an ancient kinship with brolgas. Bustards also fly with their neck and legs extended, and when walking carry themselves straight and erect with bodies parallel to the ground like a heavy, thick-necked, short-legged brolga.

what most recommended it to me. While Steve went fishing I set out on long walks, which in the wild can conjure the mystery and mysticism of a world apart. Because most visitors never hazard the unbeaten path, I had these winter-warm horizontal savannas to myself. And though alone, I wasn't lonely; I liked the solitude—it sharpened my concentration.

On my first full day's reconnaissance of the 537,000-hectare sanctuary, my attention was caught by blood-red glints of colour drifting through the tall tops of pale sorghum grasses sparkling with dew-spangled spider webs. A pair of brolgas stalked imperiously away, early light reflecting the rough red combs that contrast so conspicuously with their bare crowns of green-grey skin. Wary of my presence but irrepressibly territorial, they bugled the piercing unison call intended to repel intruders.

I encountered brolgas fairly frequently on my walks, mostly family groups or pairs lacking young and occasionally small non-breeding flocks. Parents with newly fledged chicks were shy and unrelentingly vigilant—constant threats to young lives from predators lurk everywhere. For cranes of all ages, risks increase exponentially during times of prolonged drought. Forced to abandon the home territory for an unfamiliar area, they find water, food, competitors and predators dangerously concentrated in the last shrinking wetlands.

In good years, as brolga chicks grow older the family moves further afield in their daily activities and the nesting territory becomes a home range that keeps expanding in size. As small isolated freshwater breeding swamps in the hinterland gradually dry out, families move to bigger coastal marshes dominated by bulkuru sedge. Here they join families that nested on the coast and together they form large flocks. The timing of the hinterland families' departure depends on how much rain fell during the previous wet season—the brolgas I was seeing seemed in no particular hurry to leave.

During my exploratory wanderings I was also rewarded with scattered sightings of Australia's other crane, the sarus. This enigmatic creature is closely related to the brolga, shares part of its range and, though the sarus is bigger, is often mistaken for a brolga.

Both sexes of the brolga (*Grus rubicundus*) and the Australian sarus crane (*G. antigone gilli*) have uniform aluminium-grey plumage, although the sarus is somewhat darker. Both species have bare red skin on the face, though the sarus' deeper scarlet mask extends down the neck, hence the meaning of its Wik name: 'the brolga that dipped its head in blood'. The Wik also refer to the sarus as 'the red-legged brolga' to set it apart from the true brolga, which has grey or black legs.

Other distinguishing field marks include the discreet black wattle or dewlap under the adult brolga's chin, while the sarus' concave throat is haired sparsely with small black bristles. The sarus' 'tail'—a fine bustle of plumes that are not tail feathers but the long secondary feathers of its folded wings—bends under more. The sarus' eye is reddish while the brolga's is bright yellow. Yet at a distance their appearance is sufficiently similar that they weren't formally recognised as distinct species until 1966, when the sarus was positively identified by Mrs H.B. (Billie) Gill, Eric Zillman and Fred Smith near Normanton, in the Gulf of Carpentaria.

'Saris' is a Hindi word for the call of the Indian sarus crane (*G. a. antigone*), the tallest flying bird on Earth—males may stand 1.75 metres, literally eye-to-eye with people—and one of the world's three sarus subspecies. The Indian sarus is still common in northern India but the smaller and darker eastern or Sharpe's sarus crane (*G. a. sharpii*), once abundant in South-East Asia, has been extirpated from large parts of its historic range, with an estimated 500–1500 persisting in Cambodia, Vietnam and Laos.

It was originally hypothesised that Australian sarus cranes were descended from eastern saruses that had colonised Australia relatively recently, which would account for their limited population and narrow distribution. However, the home range of the endemic Australian subspecies,[2] from Cape York Peninsula, south to Burdekin Valley and west around the Gulf of Carpentaria, is some distance from the likely point of invasion from Asia.

Cranes belong to an ancient family. Divided into two subfamilies, the African crowned cranes (Balearicinae) and the typical cranes (Gruinae), their line evolved in the age of the dinosaurs, 60–70 million years ago. The thirteen surviving Gruinae species, which includes brolgas and sarus cranes, first appear as fossils in the Miocene, 5–24 million years ago. DNA data indicates that brolgas reached Australia around

Clutching a fish headfirst to reduce drag, a father osprey returns to his family. The male will bring up to five fish a day to his chicks.

2 million years ago. The same data shows that, in terms of its phylogeny, or evolutionary history, the brolga is most closely related to the somewhat dissimilar-looking white-naped crane (*G. vipio*) of east Asia. Moreover, new mitochondrial DNA analysis suggests that the genetically distinct Australian sarus is likely descended from eastern sarus cranes that arrived in Australia nearly 40,000 years ago. So though brolgas and sarus cranes look alike, their similarities may be an example of convergent evolution, when distant relatives evolve similar traits in similar environments.

Brolgas and sarus cranes are unusual among Australia's waterbirds in that they use traditional nesting and flocking sites each year rather than being nomadic and opportunistic, as are most waterfowl. Both breed and over-winter in Lakefield, lured by the park's wet season swamps and the dry season's beautiful oases—clear pools full of flowering lilies and edged with slender, verdant umbrella sedge.

Despite having overlapping ranges, there appears to be little competition between the two crane species due to a distinct ecological separation. While bulkuru and similar wetland plants comprise the bulk of the northern brolga's diet, sarus cranes select primarily fallen seeds and other surface foods. Both breed in the late wet season, many of them in coastal wetlands around the Gulf of Carpentaria, but brolgas prefer large, long-lived swamps while sarus cranes seek out smaller wetlands in a woodland setting or parts of larger wetlands that approximate this.

The two species also manifest behavioural differences including unique vocalisations and dance and threat displays. Nevertheless, concerns have been expressed that hybridisation between brolgas and sarus cranes may be occurring. Dr George Archibald, director of the Wisconsin, USA-based International Crane Foundation and a world authority on crane biology, ecology and captive propagation has successfully interbred the two species in captivity and produced fertile offspring he dubbed 'sarolgas'. Whether hybridisation is happening in the wild, however, remains untested. Could a hybrid swarm overwhelm the biological barriers between the two species? It's anticipated that their differences will inhibit interbreeding, but it would nevertheless make a valuable and intriguing future research project.

At Lakefield, days have their own peculiar flavour—from dawn to evening the sun dictated my ways. In the cooler early mornings and late afternoons I explored a series of radiant paperbark marshes and billabongs[3] that had formed within the Normanby's catchment. During midday, when the weight of the tropical sun settled like a blanket, I relaxed unseen behind a camouflage net that I pegged between the branches of a shrub growing beside a favourite waterhole.

Waterlilies with lovely flowers—some pure white, others deep pink or magenta or blue-mauve—lent spectacular splashes of colour to the wetland scene. Waterbirds in great variety were becoming more concentrated. Fast-flying kingfishers skimmed the surface; frogs, freshwater turtles and water

OPPOSITE: *More brightly coloured than its closely related southern cousin, the tropical blue-winged kookaburra stirs up Lakefield's open eucalypt and paperbark woodlands with new-day announcements that are even more raucous than those of the laughing kookaburra. The kookaburra's long-carrying calls reinforce its territorial boundaries and explain why it is sometimes called the bushman's alarm clock.*

Moving with extreme stealth, a great egret stalks shallows
ornamented with spectacular flowering waterlilies. Belonging to
the Nymphaea *family, the waterlilies come in all shapes, colours
and sizes and grow at various depths, from the shallow swampy
edges of quiet backwaters to lagoons up to 3 metres deep.*

monitors made their living on or below it. Fairy-wrens and feeding parties of twittering finches patrolled the rank grasses that occupied the high ground. Lakefield's lily gardens were astir with a diversity of life.

By late afternoon the first feral pigs began arriving. They came in ones and twos, and sometimes in sounders of up to twenty, with striped piglets trotting in a row. The black coarsely haired adults, broad-shouldered and narrow-backed, with pricked ears and long snouts, looked more like their Eurasian wild boar cousins than the pink domestic stock from which they are descended. Folklore has it that the ancestors of the pigs I was seeing originally escaped from the Cook expedition when it put ashore at the Endeavour River. The escapees are said to have bred up to become the irascible Captain Cookers—huge, hard-bristled and curl-tusked feral hogs—that today teem throughout the peninsula.

The pigs barrelled into sight with unhesitating assurance and immediately set about churning up the edges of the lagoon in search of roots and invertebrates with the single-mindedness of earth-moving machines. The damage their rooting and wallowing causes to soil-binding vegetation is often considerable, especially when the ground is damp and seeds are set to germinate. When new seedlings are destroyed there is no regeneration of trees and shrubs to replace old plants as they die.

Pigs also destroy the nests of both aquatic and ground-dwelling birds while raiding eggs. Of all Australia's animal pests, they have the most varied impact on both the natural environment and farming.

Nationwide, pigs directly threaten a dozen species of plants and an equal number of animal species, not to mention the $200–300 million they cost agriculture annually.

Around 24 million feral pigs inhabit about 40 per cent of Australia. Since they require moist conditions, they are most abundant in the tropics, where many experts regard them as the biggest threat to the north's natural ecology. Dr Jim Mitchell, Senior Zoologist for the Tropical Weeds Research Centre told me that aerial surveys suggest Lakefield supports about twelve pigs per square kilometre. 'Mobs of 20–50 are quite normal and I've seen mobs of over 100 in the park.' Herds of up to 400 have been recorded elsewhere on the peninsula.

The control of feral pig numbers is an undertaking that is waged like a virtual war. Shooting the pigs from a helicopter is considered the most effective way of culling them in Lakefield's largely inaccessible landscape. Armed with shotguns and high-powered .308 rifles, marksmen flying a total of 62 hours dropped 2500 pigs during one recent control program in the park. Depending on the season and habitat, cost effectiveness per pig culled varies from between $4.50 per 100 pigs per hour to $26.00 per twenty pigs per hour.

Pigs are also shot on an opportunistic basis by park staff during vehicle patrols, but after years of hunting pressure some of the more aggressive would-be targets have adopted the attitude that attack is the best form of defence. 'Lakefield's pigs have got a nasty reputation,' a park ranger told me. 'One evening a couple of us were rolling out our swags when we heard a helluva

With a 'smile' as wide as that of Jabba the Hut, a green tree frog relaxes during the day on a tree beside a peaceful billabong. The enlarged pads on the tree frog's fingers and toes are coated with a sticky secretion that allows it to move about its arboreal kingdom with acrobatic ease in pursuit of a range of food items from insects to mice.

commotion in the bushes. We jumped into the back of the ute and next thing this big boar breaks cover and slams into the side of the vehicle. Then it backed up and charged again, connecting with another almighty crash.' A bullet finally put paid to the mayhem.

'You gotta watch out,' he advised me, when I told him I'd be hiking. 'If you get bailed up, get a tree trunk between you and the pig. Keep dodging until he loses interest. Usually it doesn't take too long.'

Ferals cast a broad ecological shadow over Lakefield. Wild scrub cattle straying into the park from neighbouring pastoral properties are also major offenders. The damage wrought by pigs, cattle and horses appears most vividly along Lakefield's riverbanks and around lagoons. Heavy downpours during the wet season exacerbate the erosion they cause. Following a major cattle destocking program, shrubby woodland and tall grasses along the Normanby River recovered remarkably. When beautiful Red Lily Lagoon was fenced off to prevent, among other things, egg-raiding pigs destroying crane and other waterbird nests not already trampled by cattle, it filled with aquatic plants where once there had been open water, and magpie geese have started nesting there again.

Another threat comes from pig poachers operating in the park. I saw a party of hunters outside Lakefield, their strong, sturdy dogs transported in chicken-wire cages mounted on the back of a ute. Illegal hunters set ecologically disastrous fires to clear the country but also to create a diversion, drawing rangers away to firefight at one end of the park while they chase pigs in the other. When caught and prosecuted they use arson as payback. A flame dropped into tinder-dry grass causes conflagrations 'so bad,' one ranger confided, 'that you wonder if it wouldn't be easier to let them off with a warning.'

The impact of changed fire regimes tops the list of tropical Australia's most pressing environmental challenges. I'd be taking a closer look at the science of living with fire on the northern savannas after our 600-kilometre drive south to Mareeba Wetlands, an important new crane sanctuary and our next destination.

This feral boar rooting in a Lakefield wetland is destroying soil-binding native vegetation, which in turn helps the spread of introduced weeds. Feral pigs are omnivorous feeders that not only damage habitat but also prey on protected animals—an autopsy found 303 sand frogs in one pig's stomach alone. Many experts see these prolific breeders as the biggest threat to tropical northern Australia's natural ecology; in good conditions feral pig populations can increase fivefold in a twelve-month period.

CHAPTER FOUR

Mareeba Wetlands

Once upon a time, when Emu had very long wings, she flew from her home in the sky to join Brolga dancing by a lagoon. 'You can't dance with such long wings,' said Brolga. 'Let me clip them for you.' After cutting Emu's wings very short, cunning old Brolga spread her long wings, which she had hidden by folding them along her back, and flew away. Now unable to fly, Emu never returned to her home in the sky.

—'WHY EMU HAS SHORT WINGS', ABORIGINAL CREATION STORY

It's early August in far north Queensland, well into the dry season, and though late rains have eased the parching effects of the region's annual drought, they've only slowed the ebbing of the good times. On the plains beneath the jagged Atherton Tableland's hazy blue silhouette, Mareeba Wetlands' eucalypt and paperbark parklands have assumed an autumnal ambience, full of desiccated leaves that drift down onto the ground as a breeze gusts through.

With the onset of the dry season, trees grow with difficulty, if at all. Nutrients are drawn back from the leaves to be stored underground. Survival means growing backwards in order to reduce the area requiring moisture. The tall tussocky perennial grasses produce new tissue only during the rainy season; once they mature they turn dry and stalky and lose all nutritional value. In search of green pick, wild horses attended by a coterie of cattle egrets have vacated the yellowing savanna to graze the margins of Pandanus Lagoon's waterlogged meadows. The bone-white birds hitch rides on the brumbies' backs, alighting to snatch insects disturbed by the horses' hooves, then rising to settle again.

It's an idyllic tableau and one that displays a rough but intriguing timeline of what has gone before. The Atherton Tableland's shrouded heights are the eroded remnant of an ancient highland formed around 100 million years ago when the eastern side of the Australian continental plate surged upwards, creating a mountainous escarpment. The uniquely Australian paperbarks and eucalypts—so perfectly adapted to this land that they have become synonymous with it—evolved from ancient Gondwanan stock as the continent dried while drawing closer to the equator during its 36 million years of isolation. The brumbies are wild descendants of ponies ridden by a contingent of native police picketed near here in the late 1800s. Cattle egrets—a species that once occurred naturally only in Africa and southern Europe—confounded ornithologists by following livestock to Asia and the Americas by spontaneous dispersal, and then within in a few swift decades they winged their way across the Timor Sea to Australia via Indonesia. They first appeared in the 1940s and within twenty years had spread throughout

The plump, short-tailed squatter pigeon spends most of its time on the ground, feeding mainly on seeds. Like all seed-eaters, squatter pigeons face a food shortage during the early wet season, as they rely heavily on perennial grasses whose seed production can be affected by burning in the previous dry season.

PAGES 54–5: *A pair of brolgas with their sub-adult offspring feed along the margins of Pandanus Lagoon, Mareeba Wetlands.*

OPPOSITE: *Bulbous termite mounds, some as big as a small car, are a feature of Mareeba Wetland's tropical savannas. Australia's 200 termite species build mounds of various sizes and shapes, but shapes can also vary greatly according to local conditions. Evolution in termites may have expressed itself in various mound shapes rather than variations in body form.*

agricultural Australia. The most recent advent is Pandanus Lagoon—one of a series of wetlands brought into existence by the guiding vision and energy of one man, conservationist Tim Nevard, who recognised this degraded cattle country's ecological potential and set out to fulfil it.

'When we opened in 1999 and the first brolgas turned up, it was a real red-letter day!' Tim emailed me after I got home. 'Since then, tens of thousands of people from all over the world have come to enjoy the reserve. Looking back, it seems really unbelievable, all the fuss and heartache it took to get the place up and running.'

Unfortunately, our arrival at the Mareeba Tropical Savanna and Wetland Reserve—to give it its full name—coincided with Tim's departure to the United Kingdom, where he is closely involved with the reintroduction of Eurasian cranes to England's last remaining bogs and marshes. Instead, his gracious wife Gwyneth made us welcome on our arrival at the visitor centre overlooking Clancy's Lagoon, 20 kilometres north-west of Mareeba township.

We sat on the timber deck while overhead welcome swallows attended their adobe nests among the rafters, where at night ghost bats and epauletted bats rest between insect-hunting forays across the lagoon. Gwyneth passed around mugs of good strong coffee and homemade cookies. 'Tim's inspiration to create a wetland reserve had plenty of sceptics,' she noted with a touch of pride. 'But he never stopped believing it would happen.'

Originally this 2000-hectare parcel of land, situated at the end of the now-obsolete Cape York Peninsula stock route, was earmarked for sugarcane production but its complex soils and geological composition proved unsuitable for intensive agriculture. After an in-depth environmental investigation, Tim, as head of the non-profit Mareeba Wetland Foundation, proposed using surplus water from the nearby Mareeba–Dimbulah irrigation scheme to create an ecosystem of gravity-fed wetlands set within a tropical savanna. The year was 1994; ahead lay a tough five-year battle to bring that dream to fruition.

'When we started the project, we were assailed from all sides,' Tim recalled. With water a precious commodity in a region with limited supplies and growing demand, 'some farmers complained we were

Proffering a token of green fruit, a highly excited male great bowerbird hopes to entice a female inspecting his carefully tended bower. Used only for display and mating, the constantly refurbished bower comprises a half-metre-long avenue of woven twigs and grasses. The male places his artfully arranged collection of white pebbles, bones and bleached snail shells in a cleared space at each end. All this effort advertises his reproductive fitness to a passing female.

getting it for free while they had to pay—claimed we got special treatment because we're greenies. It got them as spitting angry as a stepped-on snake. One fellow publicly threatened to shoot me! He "knew for a fact" that there was no such thing as unused overflow water exiting the end of the channel system, water that was fuelling the reserve's dangerously growing biodiversity! When another irrigator told him this occurs in all open-channel irrigation areas, it only seemed to inflame him more.'

The farmers' howls of protest were just the beginning: 'The greenies thought we were too close to the farmers and not really interested in nature conservation,' Tim discovered. 'They implied we had a hidden agenda to use the wetlands as a ruse to extend the irrigation area. Politicians of all persuasions accused us of being too close to the other side, and the tourism industry said the reserve wasn't being properly developed as a nature-based tourism destination because we were too quiet about it, keeping our heads down to avoid brickbats from farmers, greenies and would-be pollies!'

Performing his extravagant courtship display, a male great bowerbird flares the lilac crest on his nape, flicks his head and gapes to reveal his yellow mouth while letting loose a rapturous barrage of hisses, churrs, gratings, twangs and rasps. He is an accomplished mimic, copying the calls of a variety of other birds as well as noises of human origin, such as a squeaking gate or cracking stockwhip.

Then, just as the earthworks were nearing completion in early 1999, Cyclone Rona struck, causing Clancy's Lagoon to burst its banks. Despite the setback, repairs and all major construction were completed in May that year. The twelve separate lagoons, connected by creeks and channels, immediately began attracting a wild profusion of aquatic life.

With his bulldog drive and pugnacity, no one is better suited to weathering the winds of the conservationist's arcane world, with all its swirling controversies, than Tim, says Gwyneth with a wife's hard-won lucidity. Tim brings to the task a rare breed of self-confidence and an unflinching sense of who he is and where he's going. Ultimately he was able to get through to and move even the most diverse and multi-sectoral audience.

Support began gathering momentum, from the Commonwealth and state governments, from the local community—particularly conservation and naturalist organisations and the shire council and local businesses—and from sponsors such as the Australian Geographic Society. Walking tracks were laid, trees planted and weeds eradicated during a six-month GreenCorps program. As the wildlife increased, the tourism industry wholeheartedly embraced the project, supporting further funding under the Regional Tourism Program.

These days, Mareeba Wetlands is home to twenty mammal and 40 reptile species, as well as 204 species of birds, including the very rare buff-breasted button quail. Situated as it is on the East Asian/Australasian flyway, the reserve offers a place for long-distance migrants to stop over and refuel. Crucially, the reserve's primary mission to become prime waterbird habitat has been a spectacular success, and it is now one of the more important brolga and sarus crane roosts in Australia.

By way of introduction to the reserve, its warden, Craig Mills, a lean and wiry biologist and micro-bat specialist with wide experience in habitat management, invited me on a sunrise cruise the following morning. We cast off in the silent electric-motor boat he uses to take paying visitors on tours of Clancy's Lagoon. At that early hour we had the place to ourselves. Long

Mareeba Wetlands' warden, Craig Mills, navigates sublime Clancy's Lagoon. Hann Tableland is in the background.

With eyes and skills as sharp as its beak, a white-bellied sea eagle waits on a favoured perch for a fish to rise in the lagoon below. When an opportunity presents, the eagle descends in a long, fast glide and, relying on split-second timing, snatches its prey from the surface with a sweep of its huge, hooked talons. At the moment of strike, this specialist hunter is at full stall and, with the added weight of the snagged fish, it requires enormous strength to take off again before sinking. This display is aided by small spikes on the bottom of the sea eagle's feet, which help it to grasp slippery prey.

trails of mist blanketed the lagoon but the sun was coming and would soon burn it off—already its trajectory was glinting off stone in the high Hann Tableland to the west.

The pink flush in the sky turned to gold, etching golden streaks into the lagoon's flat black surface. Out on the water time was slow and the peace and harmony filled me with wellbeing. The air was so still that I could hear sounds from a long way off—the nasal groans of Torresian crows plotting in the winter woodlands; the quick *pop-pop* of feeding fish. On this languid, delicate morning everything seemed to exult in living.

Across the pond a great crested grebe skittered over lotus pads, and ducking beneath the skin of the water—sleek, soundlessly—disappeared into the blackness. A lone pelican—awkwardly shaped, heavy-bodied, heavy-billed, with no balancing length of tail—flew low above the glittering water. A yellow-eyed female black-necked stork with ruby-coloured legs probed the water snowflake-decorated shallows with a cleaver bill sturdy enough to open a can of tuna; the pearly light reflected water dripping from her shiny sable bill. Beside the edge of the quiet pond a crowd of wandering whistling ducks stood doing nothing very much. There came the pipe of coots and the scattering slap of their runs across the surface, and the morning flight of doves to water. At that magic hour there seemed something almost primeval about this place. These scenes have been repeated, day after day, through the millennia. That they were happening here, where until recently there was only a dusty plain, seemed a small miracle.

I broke off my reverie to take a closer look at this community of wild animals, for there are finely balanced ecological processes at work here. Waterbird abundance is dependent on the availability of suitable wetland habitat. Not just any area of water will do—value is determined by food availability. Different habitats provide different foods and because many waterbirds have specific diets, species vary between habitat types. A permanent wetland like Clancy's Lagoon supports fish and so is favoured by fish-eating species.

Craig pointed out a silent scattering of piscivorous birds at work; in turn, we were closely watched by a white-bellied sea eagle poised atop a paperbark, just sitting there, looking magnificent. Long-legged waders—herons, egrets, spoonbills, stilts—gathered in the shallows, stalking, probing, striking, straining fish and frogs. I watched an intermediate egret—a stealthy, pitiless-eyed hunter able to spot the slightest stirrings underwater—trail its plumes in the mire while somehow maintaining their alabaster perfection.

Suddenly the head and kinked neck of a darter broke the surface with the forthrightness of a periscope. In common with cormorants, darters have permeable plumage that reduces their buoyancy, allowing them to sink easily. Unlike cormorants that 'fly' underwater in pursuit of their prey, a submerged darter stalks fish with the stealth, frozen posture—serpentine, highly articulated neck drawn back into a S-shape—and sudden swift stab that the egret uses out of water. The next time the darter surfaced he had an eel-tailed catfish impaled on his dagger-like bill. With a shake of his head he tossed the fish into the air, caught it and swallowed it head-first to avoid injury from spiny fins and barbs.

Later I saw the replete bird perched on a stump, hanging his glossy black and silver streaked plumage out to dry on widespread wings, a stance that also aids digestion.

A boat-habituated family of comb-crested jacanas strode with splay-footed assurance across a mat of tilting and sliding lotus leaves in search of insects and seeds. Popularly known as lily trotters or lotus birds, these specialised waders have extraordinarily long toes—the longest, relative to body size, of any bird in the world. The birds' elongated toes and long straight claws spread their weight, enabling them to pick their way across floating water plants almost as if they're walking on water—which accounts for another nickname: Jesus bird.

From the south, shortly after sun-up, a sarus crane's distinctive two-note *garrraww* contact call wafted in—deeper and more rolling than the brolga's voice—followed by the birds themselves, brolgas as well as sarus cranes, crossing the sky in broken strings, the low sun burnishing the edges of their wings. They approached with slow, powerful wingbeats, their outstretched necks undulating slightly as they turned their heads to stare down at us as they passed. The elegant Quaker-grey birds were commuting from their communal roost at Pandanus Lagoon to nearby irrigated farmlands where harvest waste provides an opportune food supply to tide them over the lean winter months.

As their wet season billabongs and shallow sedgelands on the Gulf of Carpentaria's south-eastern subcoastal plains begin to recede, many cranes become locally migratory, with an October peak of some 400–600 regularly over-wintering at Mareeba Wetlands. The several hundred kilometre journey from the Gulf is undertaken mostly by day to take advantage of the warm thermals. Travelling cranes use 'spiral-gliding' flight where possible to save energy by riding the air currents. Watching them sometimes means straining to see high, distant specks—pilots have reported flocks at 3600 metres.

With the spread of row crops in northern Queensland, a substantial portion of the sarus crane and brolga populations have adapted their feeding habits to human agricultural activity. They've come to depend on harvest gleanings during the dry season and prefer to roost within easy flying distance of croplands. Although not all of Mareeba Wetlands' cranes make the daily flight to neighbouring farms—some remain behind and forage for more traditional fare such as high-energy sedge tubers—those that do are, by and large, tolerated by the landowners. In return, the cranes eat useful quantities of pasture pests like crickets and grasshoppers. Confronted by the all-consuming tidal wave of modern human culture, some cranes have accommodated—even benefited from—the new order, and it's to the great credit of local farmers that they have extended neighbourly goodwill towards these annual gatherings.

But not all bird species have made such a smooth transition to changed habitats. Just 50 years ago highly social flocks of brilliantly coloured Gouldian finches flourished in the millions across Australia's grassy northern savannas from Cape York Peninsula through the Top End of the

Fishing at first light, a darter surfaces with an eel-tailed catfish impaled on its needle-sharp bill. The darter will swallow its catch headfirst to avoid being pierced by the catfish's venomous dorsal and pectoral fin spines, which cause great pain if they puncture the skin.

Northern Territory to the Kimberley region of Western Australia. Today these Australian endemics persist in only a handful of fragmented sites. With a present total population conservatively estimated at about 2500 mature individuals at the start of the breeding season—less than the world's wild tiger population—this most boldly plumaged of the grassfinches has become another grim addition to the endangered species list.

The dire situation was first recognised in the 1980s, when WWF Australia played a leading role in much-needed ecological research and the drafting of the first national Gouldian finch recovery plan. More recently, the Mareeba Wetland Foundation, in collaboration with the Queensland Parks and Wildlife Service and James Cook University, as well as local amateur aviculturists, has established a breed-and-release program which aims to reintroduce Gouldians to the Mareeba Wetlands, where they have been absent for 25 years.

Soon after my arrival, I was introduced to Julia Deleyev, a thoughtful, self-contained young ornithologist in charge of special projects. Her varied duties include the supervision of the reserve's Gouldian finch restocking program. Those Gouldians destined for release are housed in two aviaries on the property. However, Julie acknowledges that there are inherent problems involved in setting free descendants of birds bred in captivity for up to 25 generations.

'They're great favourites with bird-breeders,' she told me. 'There must be tens of thousands of them in cages around the world. Trouble is, wild animals bred in captivity are prone to genetic drift.' Selective breeding has produced in Gouldians a high incidence of colour imbalances and mutations not found in any wild population.

In the wild, adult male Gouldians have brighter plumage than females, otherwise they both have grass-green backs, blue upper-tail coverts, a yellow belly and a lilac breast band. This kaleidoscope of colours not-withstanding, their most arresting feature is their crown and face mask, which is black in 70–80 per cent of the population; dull crimson in 20–30 per cent; with a few ochre-yellow rarities, the result of lack of pigmentation in red-faced birds. In some captive breeding circles where the unusual is prized, this ratio is often reversed, potentially leading to an ever-widening genetic gulf between captive and wild populations. Julie is determined to ensure that released birds are genetically compatible with any wild survivors.

Another concern regarding the wild release of captive-bred birds is their ability to make a living and evade predators. When not breeding, free-ranging Gouldian finches feed for the most part on ripe or half-ripe grass seeds; their short, conical beaks are perfectly adapted for processing hard grass seeds. They are also expert at catching flying termite nymphs in mid-air, and during the breeding season they become almost entirely insectivorous, nurturing their chicks on this protein-rich diet.

However, while feeding they must also safeguard against becoming food themselves. Most birds instinctively recognise and flee their enemies but instinct may become dangerously dulled if not fired by parental

Big flocks of gregarious chestnut-breasted mannikins clamber nimbly among Mareeba Wetlands' banks of tall grasses while feeding on half-ripe grass seeds. Mannikins and Gouldian finches both feed by pulling down an upright grass stem and then clamping it with one foot while they pick out the seeds. The two species often form mixed feeding parties and flock together to visit waterholes, where lurking predators make safety in numbers a wise precaution.

example. After generations of cage living, would reintroduced Gouldians be able to cope in a food chain that ultimately divides into the quick and the dead?

In March 2002, twenty drab-grey immature Gouldian finches were transported in a mobile aviary to the far side of Clancy's Lagoon. What followed was a classic 'soft' release. With a supplemental supply of grain on offer in the release pen, the door was left open and the birds allowed to come and go at their own pace. Within the first half-hour of freedom they began feeding on native grasses that they had never before encountered.

Later they teamed up with a flock of chestnut-breasted mannikins and, just like mannikins and wild-born Gouldians, they were soon climbing and clinging to vertical grass stalks to pick out seeds, rather than foraging on the ground. Some instincts, it seems, never die, although staying out of the clutches of predators would prove much harder to do.

The supplemental feeding attracted other seed-eaters such as double-barred finches and Julie was able to observe their hair-trigger flight response when a raptor appeared, whereas the Gouldians 'hung around and got nailed'. A further two releases in 2003 were also targeted by a guild of predators including collared sparrowhawks and brown goshawks, pied butcherbirds, northern quolls and brown tree snakes. Past experience with animals raised in captivity, with little or no natural experience—such as the reintroduction of black-footed ferrets and whooping cranes in the United States—has shown that a high mortality seems unavoidable until a few individuals learn to survive the rigours of the wild and pass on their hard-won wisdom to offspring. So staff were excited to receive news in July 2004 that a small flock of two adult and up to sixteen juvenile Gouldian finches had been seen by experienced birders at Big Mitchell Creek, 20 kilometres north of the reserve.

'That gave us real hope that we were on the right track,' Tim Nevard reported in *Jabiru*, the foundation's newsletter. 'These birds had survived and bred in the wild.' Tim is determined to succeed. 'We've learnt massive amounts about the successful rearing, radio-tracking and subsequent monitoring of our finches. Part of our future strategy includes expanded breeding facilities in order to release bigger numbers, thereby swamping the local predators.'

Before any finches could be released, however, it was essential to understand what had caused their precipitous population crash in the first place. Initially, the finger of blame was pointed at trapping for the aviary trade, which was permitted until the late 1980s, but scientists doubt that a bird which lays a clutch of four to eight eggs and can rear two to three broods in a good year could have been so disastrously over-harvested. The Gouldian's decline, recent studies have shown, has parallelled that of other

OPPOSITE: *These brilliantly coloured Gouldian finches are part of Mareeba Wetlands' reintroduction program. Recent sightings of flocks of hundreds of Gouldians in places where they have not been seen for up to fifteen years has researchers hoping that, due to better fire management, one of Australia's most endangered birds could be on the road to recovery.*

granivorous birds in northern Australia's tropical savannas, including star finches and crimson finches that were once widespread on Cape York Peninsula. Seed-eating birds are in more trouble than any other animal group in the savannas, and savanna seed-eaters are in more trouble than those elsewhere in Australia. Research has shown that a common theme in the savanna seed-eaters' decline is a changed fire regime in their grassland ecosystem.[1]

The ecology of fire to manage the landscape is very ancient. No other human technology has influenced the planet for so long and so pervasively. Over their 50,000-plus years of occupation, the Aboriginal peoples' annual 'firestick farming' helped 'clean up the country', facilitating travel and improving visibility for the mobile hunter-gatherers, particularly in dense grasslands. Fires allow landscapes to renew and reinvigorate themselves by recycling nutrients from wood, grass and undecomposed litter back into the impoverished soil.

Removing matted old plant growth also improves nesting conditions for the magpie geese that supplied Aboriginal people with meat and eggs. To the modern city-dweller, fires may suggest death and destruction but for the hunters this seeming devastation presaged the forthcoming season of green when the rains would come again, producing a flush of fresh growth that would attract wallabies and make them easier targets for their spears.

Historical records show that in the past Aboriginal people set fires almost any time it wasn't raining. The steady removal of fuel kept wild fires in check and resulted in a complex environmental mosaic of small burnt and unburnt patches that left pockets of seed at different stages of maturity to sustain seed-eaters throughout the year. Without active patch-burn management, extensive wild fires consume vast areas and have the potential to burn adjacent fire-sensitive areas.

'Pastoralism radically changed traditional fire regimes,' Craig Mills said as we drove out one warm and windless late afternoon to set a controlled burn behind Clancy's Lagoon. Most graziers opted for occasional, widespread dry-season fires, he explained, which led to a uniform, homogenised habitat

Possessing the largest feet and toes relative to body size of any bird in the world, the comb-crested jacana is able to walk lightly across floating lily pads and other water weeds as it probes for insects, snails, aquatic plants and seeds. The pigment in the jacana's fleshy comb is yellow—the red comes from circulating blood. If the jacana becomes excited during courtship or danger the blood flow is restricted and the colour changes from red to yellow.

over an extensive area, severely limiting the amount of food available to wildlife. The result: more bird species are threatened by altered fire regimes today than by any other factor except for land clearing.

Open grassy plains, one of the brolga's preferred natural habitats, are being altered dramatically over parts of far north Queensland by changed fire-management practices. After four or more years with no fire or only early dry-season burns, tropical savannas risk invasion by woody plants, in particular the broad-leaved paperbark (*Melaleuca viridiflora*), which sprouts suckers from its base that can spread in great abundance. The resulting conversion of grassland to dense woodland affects cranes and a whole suite of other bird species, including bustards and the endangered golden-shouldered parrot, by cutting out light, thus reducing grass growth and the birds' food resources. Only very hot, late dry-season fires called storm burns, lit just before the rains come when fuel levels are high, will keep re-suckering paperbarks below grass height. To save and perhaps restore valuable open grasslands, attempts are now underway to start a fire mosaic that includes hot, seasonal burns.[2]

For Gouldian finches—dependent on seed from a select few perennial grass species, all of which may be in short supply at the onset of the wet season depending on previous seasons' fire and rainfall—the changes meant starvation. Moreover, the stress of seed shortages made them susceptible to infection by the air sac mite parasite, although it's not considered a major cause of their decline.

When to burn and when not to burn is a hot topic among land managers. Craig recognises the need for well-directed, limited-area hot burns to control invasive woody plants, though generally he prefers cool, patchy August fires that don't spread too far or last too long. Burning in the evening means the heavy dew at this time of year suppresses fire intensity, creating a wavy edged, fine-scale mosaic of vegetation types akin to traditional Aboriginal burning patterns.

Early the next morning I returned to the burn site. At the sight and sound of my vehicle, a pair of sarus cranes broke off feeding to monitor my approach. Many bird species, including cranes and finches, track fires across the landscape to feed on grass seeds—protected by fire-resistant outer coats—and insects made more visible and accessible by the removal of the dense grass cover.

The cessation of cattle grazing in the reserve means grasses will have the opportunity to set seed. Combined with sustainable fire management practices and feral pig control measures, there is now a real chance to restore the habitat. At Mareeba Wetlands, the Gouldian finch shares the brolga's mantle of umbrella species. Securing its former range will benefit a suite of other seed-eating birds as well as declining native mammal and plant species of the northern savannas.

The next day I would continue south to lush Atherton Tableland, where radically altered habitats, created by bush clearing rather than fire, are presenting opportunities for brolgas, but severe challenges for the region's long-established wild residents.

The sun drops below the horizon, firing Clancy's Lagoon with the brief splendour of twilight and silhouetting little pied cormorants as they settle for the night. It is a scene that has been repeated in wild Australia, year after year. That it should be happening here, in Mareeba Wetlands, is a tribute to the dedication of a handful of wildlife conservationists.

CHAPTER FIVE

Cranes in the Mist

This noble and princely creature [is] most delighted to live in fenny places, lakes, and standing pools or ryvers … Their flesh is profitable against cancers, ulcers, palsies, and wind in the guts … The brains have been used against sores in the seat … And the fat of cranes (said Pliny) mollifies hard swellings and tuberous bunches.

—EDWARD TOPSELL, *THE FOWLES OF HEAVEN*, 1614

Brolgas wade long-legged among drowned eucalypts at Mandalee Swamp.

PAGES 74–5: *The ghostly shapes of brolgas shrouded in winter marsh mist emerge from the grey daybreak.*

The early winter morning at Mandalee Swamp was pale and serene; a dense fog overlaid still waters. Heads beneath their wings, the ghostly one-legged shapes of roosting cranes stood hunched in a forest of drowned trees. Sleeping while standing in ankle-deep water provides a defence against mammalian predators—the wary birds can hear or perhaps feel the ripples made by an approaching enemy. Indeed, it was so quiet I could hear my own breathing.

On a grey August dawn I watched as light filtered dimly through marsh mist to reveal the mysteriously shifting silhouettes of waking brolgas. By 8 a.m. the risen sun was strong enough to lift the mist like wisps and strands of smoke, creating a diffused fiery glow that tinted Mandalee's shallow water a tawny gold. The brolgas feather-shifted and preened, and flared their wings in preparation for the day ahead. Suddenly a big male, his wings arched, threw back his head, aimed his bill skyward and uttered a whooping staccato clarion. A female, standing alongside in the same posture except for wings folded at her side, immediately answered with a rapid two or three calls for each of his. The mated pair's wild antiphonal unison duet, audible for up to 5 kilometres, set the working day in motion as one family group after another took flight, crossing the winter sky in unhurried echelons.

That morning over a thousand brolgas and possibly a few sarus cranes departed Mandalee Swamp for neighbouring broad brown stubble fields to glean corn left over from the harvest. By midmorning Mandalee becomes a 'loafing' area and most cranes return to drink, preen and indulge in social displays. Later that afternoon they would again feed in the stubble fields before once more returning to Mandalee, this time to roost in its flooded pastures.

This 12-hectare marsh on a cattle station near the small southern Atherton Tableland township of Innot Hot Springs provided me with the most spectacular concentration of cranes I saw on my travels. As the dry season advanced, the ash-grey legions would increase to as many as 2000 as other, more ephemeral wetlands dried out.

Astonishingly, Mandalee Swamp is wholly artificially created. In 1972 an embankment was bulldozed to block wet-season drainage, creating a simple

Against the backdrop of a pivot irrigator and green fields of standing corn, brolgas glean the stubble near Innot Hot Springs for corn left over from the autumn harvest.

but very effective dam. Over time aquatic plants colonised the waterlogged land, which during the dry season rarely exceeds a metre in depth—perfect habitat for bustling populations of cranes, swans, ducks, geese, grebes and crakes.

Steve Nott and I had been invited here by fellow wildlife enthusiasts Jan O'Sullivan and Arthur Palmer, residents of Cairns who grab every opportunity to take a few days off from their busy schedules and go bush. Both are volunteers with Birds Australia-North Queensland Group (BA-NQG).

Founded in 1901 as the Royal Australasian Ornithologists' Union, Birds Australia—with its more than 7000 members—is nowadays a hands-on scientific organisation that, among its many activities, sponsors conservation-based research projects. In 1997, its north Queensland branch initiated a long-term investigation into the number and distribution of cranes over-wintering on the tableland.

Each year in early October over 100 volunteer birdwatchers, coordinated by ornithologist Elinor Scambler, assemble at all known major roost sites from Townsville to Mareeba and west to Mount Garnet to count the thousands of brolgas and sarus cranes flying in for the night. Since 1999, when they first discovered it, Jan, Arthur and their friend, Eleanor Duignan, have done the count at Mandalee.

Cranes appear to be relative newcomers to the Atherton Tableland, beneficiaries of altered landscapes brought about by land clearing. By the 1890s, pioneer settlers had begun transforming the vast green waves of unbroken rainforest that had occupied much of the tableland since the end of the last ice age, 10,000 years ago, into the forest islands surrounded by cultivated fields we see today. While many species suffered as a consequence of the changes, others prospered. The first brolgas arrived following agricultural expansion, exploiting the new food sources possibly as early as 1900. Today their descendants feed in cornfields where jungles once stood.

There are few published papers documenting changing brolga[1] and sarus crane population size, trends, distribution and land use, so the BA-NQG census will help fill a significant gap. Brolgas still occupy much of their historic range in Australia's northern wet/dry tropics and, to a far lesser extent, in the southern temperate regions. (They also occur in Papua New

- Brolga distribution
- Brolga breeding sites

LEFT: *Jan O'Sullivan and Arthur Palmer canoeing on Mandalee Swamp.*

BELOW: *Unsettled by the canoe's approach, magpie geese in Mandalee Swamp flush noisily into the air with querulous honks of displeasure.*

Despite his rich purple crown and fiery collar, the male superb fruit dove's predominantly green plumage makes him hard to see when perched immobile high in an Atherton Tableland rainforest canopy. It is the dove's distinctive advertising call—a series of resonant whoops, each pitched higher than the last—that draws attention, and the sound of falling fruit as he feeds.

Guinea's southern lowlands where flocks of up to 600 have been recorded in the Trans-Fly River valley. The Sepik River Basin may support a smaller northern population, though there are no recent records.) However, a lack of systematic, wide-range surveys in northern Australia has made population estimates highly unreliable. Several northern sites are known to hold seasonal concentrations of thousands of brolgas. In total, 20,000 is presumed to be the minimum for the species but they may number 100,000 or more—even reasonable estimates should be regarded essentially as guesswork at this point.

Sarus cranes were first recorded on the Atherton Tableland in 1967, when 23 birds were sighted. Over four decades that population has increased to become the only known major dry season concentration in Australia. Although some observers infer an overall sarus population increase based on the tableland increase, Elinor Scambler has seen no detectable increase or decrease since BA-NQG started counting in 1997.

What is certain is that deforestation, followed by the spread of grazing and agricultural lands, allowed sarus cranes to dramatically increase their range beyond traditional grassland niches. In the wet/dry tropics it is often meagre dry season resources that limit wildlife populations. During his groundbreaking 1970s field study of far north Queensland brolgas, biologist and waterbird specialist Gavin Blackman reported that dead cranes were often encountered during the April to November dry season, the majority of them the young of the year. These days corn plantings and their harvest waste serve as a dependable winter resource and graziers' freshwater impoundments also help tide cranes over the arid months.

The October crane counts on the tableland and its periphery showed a remarkably consistent 'landed' minimum of about 1700 sarus until 2000, which yielded a bumper tally of 2991. Which begged the question: where did the extra birds come from? The departure of adult sarus cranes for their breeding grounds varies from year to year, so perhaps the census-takers hit the jackpot with a pre-migration peak—a few days later practically no adult birds could be found. Or perhaps the extra birds turned up from the Gulf of Carpentaria or Cape York Peninsula. Due to their remoteness these vast areas

BELOW: *The male satin bower bird decorates his avenue bower with just about any bright-blue object, including fruit, flowers, feathers, clothes pegs, bottle tops, straws and pens, as long as it complements his glossy blue-black plumage and sapphire blue eyes.*

BOTTOM: *The urgency to protect the last of Australia's wet tropical rainforests is exemplified by the fate of the endangered southern cassowary. Forest clearance and fragmentation in this bioregion has reduced cassowaries to ten isolated sub-populations; ornithologists fear that the last 2000 could decrease by 20 per cent over the next 20 years.*

have been poorly surveyed. As a result, the total Australian sarus crane population is presently uncertain, with estimates ranging from 5000 individuals to 10,000 breeding pairs plus young and 'floaters'.

The counts are also providing valuable data on roost habitat and pre-roosting movement patterns. Using GIS,[2] crane numbers and movements can be mapped in space and time, and seen in context with habitat modification resulting from rainfall, wetland water levels or changing land use. 'Flyovers' on crane count evenings can be checked for black holes, such as: is a key roost being missed?

Crane dynamics are at their most intriguing on these uplands. While brolgas outnumber sarus cranes in the drier woodlands and croplands north and west of the tableland—such as occur at Mandalee Swamp—records suggest that since the early 1980s sarus cranes have gradually become dominant on the wetter eastern and southern tableland. No one knows why. Perhaps in the future new crops and farming practices may lead to yet

more changes in the range and numbers of these enigmatic birds.

'Combining the October roost count with a simultaneous aerial count of scattered cranes in the Gulf Country and Cape York will provide a far more comprehensive population estimate,' Elinor Scambler enthused as she welcomed me with a firm and warm handshake to the PowerPoint presentation she was giving at Innot Hot Springs' atmospheric pub. Besides dedicated crane enthusiasts and counters, her audience included an encouraging community cross-section of landowners and other locals interested in issues ranging from catchment areas and sustainable agriculture to icon birds.

'It looks like a combined count is on for 2005!' Elinor was delighted to announce. Atherton Tableland resident John Grant—who has been studying the ecology and demography of sarus cranes since 1996— and Rob Heinson would coincide their annual Gulf aerial survey with Birds Australia's ground count. 'I'm still trying to get helpers for the peninsula,' Elinor said. 'Trouble is, so far we've only found one notable roost there, near Lakeland Downs. Maybe the others are so remote no one knows their location.'

Though gentle and soft-spoken, this engaging, intelligent and fiercely energetic woman has an air of quiet authority that reveals the steel-willed conservationist she is. There is something almost poignant in her avidity for the eco-friendly projects she

The first rays of the sun touch Bromfield Swamp's uplands; its volcanic crater is a bowl of thick fog.

LEFT: *Droplets of mist spangle a spider's web. In these highlands, moisture in fog and clouds is captured on leaves and stored, providing crucial water for wildlife during the dry season.*

BELOW: *Ignoring a grazing cow, sarus cranes walk up Bromfield's crater wall before departing to feed in agricultural fields a short flight away. Towards dusk, they return to roost.*

champions. A proposed regional Natural Resource Management (NRM) plan that sets out, she says, to subsidise or coerce landowners into fencing off their wetlands had aroused her misgivings. A worried look like a shadow crossed her face. 'I'm very concerned this will be done in cost-cutting mode without any thought given to the danger of large birds like cranes and black-necked storks getting killed in collisions or entanglements with fences. Also, if fences are too close to the water, birds could be "locked out", without space to land and take off unless the wetland or dam is very shallow and they can land right in it.'

Her concerns prompted Elinor to draft an evolving Crane-friendly Fencing guideline. 'I've been getting really good feedback from some catchment groups and farmers as well as Department of Primary Industries people and others like bat people who are finding bats and birds caught up in Natural Heritage Trust-funded fences,' she later emailed me.

'NRM's objectives should be tailored to the wetland's origins—whether artificial or modified-natural—and their often multiple uses,' Elinor insisted. 'It's worth remembering that most tableland crane roosts wouldn't exist without farm management that maintains them for production rather than biodiversity.' As a working farmer Elinor is perfectly positioned to appreciate both sides of the conservation-versus-development debate.

The day after meeting with Elinor, Steve and I headed north on the Kennedy Highway en route to new crane destinations in the green heart of the high country. We stopped to take on supplies at the quiet village of Ravenshoe on the western edge of the tableland. At an altitude of 915 metres, this is the highest town in Queensland. Valuable red cedar was discovered here in 1881, and in 1889 the first sawmill was built to process the timber. A century later this once busy logging community was in the forefront of a bitter, losing battle to prevent World Heritage listing of the Wet Tropics. Tragically, by the time World Heritage was ratified, over 90 per cent of the

Large-eyed and silent, a green ringtail possum stares from its realm in the lower canopy of a dense high-altitude rainforest in the Atherton Tableland. After a day spent sleeping on an exposed branch, this primitive, solitary possum becomes active an hour or two before dusk when it feeds on leaves, in particular those of the fig tree and mulberry stinging tree.

Atherton Tableland's original rainforest, wet sclerophyll forest, open woodlands and savanna grasslands had already been cleared.

We next turned north-east onto the Old Palmerston Highway, a winding, scenic detour to Millaa Millaa, a place of picturesque waterfalls and extinct shield volcanoes long since eroded to undulating hills. Seen from this gently meditative countryside, remnant pockets of deep-green forest had a dark impenetrable look, dense with lushness.

On an earlier visit to far north Queensland, the Cairns-based Wait-A-While ecotourism company had invited me on a complimentary spotlighting trip to misty Mount Baldy State Forest, a closed montane forest, 1107 metres above sea level. Even though this is the tropics, at that altitude in mid-July the evening had a chilly edge to it. It had rained, then cleared during the late afternoon and the air was spiced with the scent of wet earth and leaf rot. A stream of sulphur-crested cockatoos in careening flight announced sunset with terrible cries as they passed close above the treetops. Cattle egrets hunched like still white growths on the outer edge of a forest wall turning black with loss of light.

Night had fallen by the time our little party of clients and I, led by tour guide Ben Blewitt, left the vehicle and set out on foot along a firebreak that cut like a dead straight canyon through towering trees. Fallen leaves quilted the track. Through the gap in the canopy directly above us, the stars were sharp points of light. Luminescent fungi shone dimly in the shadows.

Silently we walked in single file, Ben's beam casting a bright pool of light down the muddy track, briefly showing the way ahead, then flicking searchingly up looming tree trunks that looked in the sub-aqueous glow like grey columns in a Gothic cathedral. Somewhere in the night a dingo called with long-winded insistence, tremblingly high like a melancholy flautist. From further up the track came the falling-bomb screams of a lesser sooty owl.

Over the millennia, the tableland's densely forested slopes and hidden valleys gave rise to their own patterns of life. Possums evolved in rainforests and the earliest species still live here, little changed from their forebears. Early evening is the best time to look for them, when foraging is at its peak.

We began encountering some of the more common species before we had gone far—their bright eyeshine an instant giveaway.

Easiest to spot were Daintree River ringtails, attracted to the road by their fondness for the leaves of trees that grow beside clearings. Caught in the beam, the possum would freeze, peering down at us from the overstorey with a mild, somewhat bemused expression on its face, its strong prehensile tail coiled securely around a branch. Coppery brushtails—a reddish tropical subspecies of the common brushtail—were also relatively plentiful, as were green ringtails, probably the most primitive ancestral form of possum still living. The spotlight picked out an occasional dark-phase lemuroid ringtail, a species endemic to north-east Queensland rainforests over 450 metres above sea level and which occur at their highest density along the summits of mountain ranges like Mount Baldy. I was also able to add the handsome Herbert River ringtail to my personal checklist, and though hoping to include the strikingly marked, insect-eating striped possum, the only one seen that night was a forlorn roadkill lying beside the paved road back to Cairns.

A high point of the evening's viewing was a single Lumholtz's tree-kangaroo, squatting flat-footed on a branch, its long, dark furry tail hanging down. These extraordinary creatures probably evolved from a primitive, ground-dwelling kangaroo—itself evolved from an arboreal ancestor—that gradually readapted to life aloft. Unlike possums, a tree-kangaroo's tail is not prehensile but only acts as a counterbalance for these clumsy climbers. Also, unlike the possums we'd seen, the tree-kangaroo seemed agitated by our presence. Ben turned off his spotlight, concerned that the shy animal—perhaps responding to an atavistic memory of Aboriginal hunting—might leap from its high perch and injure or even kill itself, as they have been known to do. We left quietly, anxious to avoid causing harm.

On this trip I bypassed the forests, instead driving 8 kilometres south-west of historic Malanda township to Bromfield Swamp, a well-known night roost for up to 800 sarus cranes and 200 brolgas. Like nearby lakes Eacham and Barrine, Bromfield is a maar—a geological term for a volcanic crater blasted into existence by a single massive explosion when confined water became super-heated by rising magma. Many maars contain crater lakes but at Bromfield the ring wall has been breached by erosion and drained to become a shallow swamp and an ideal roost for cranes.

Friends of Jan O'Sullivan's had earlier offered us the hospitality of their farmhouse, though they would be away. Perched on Bromfield's northern rim and directly overlooking the circular 60-metre deep caldera, their home's back verandah provided a spectacular viewing platform. The dead volcano's floor was set about with peaty pools bordered by reeds, sedges, rushes, grasses and dwarf paperbarks; the crater walls, largely cleared of rainforest, were covered with grassy pastures kept cropped by cattle.

From below, amplified by the crater, came the hiss of the breeze disturbing the sedge and a sudden beating of wings against water which subsided abruptly.

Plumed whistling ducks at Hasties Swamp drink by scooping up water with their bill and letting it run down their throat. The whistling sound made by their wings in flight and their shrill, high-pitched calls account for this handsome duck's name.

Early arrivals, mostly brolgas, were already landed. As the sun gave way to the gloaming, bugle notes from the heavens signalled the approach of more cranes—separate flocks of brolgas and sarus arriving in long columns or arrowhead V-formations. They dropped in slow against the breeze, the brolga's deeper, more raucous call distinct from the low rolling greeting a sarus utters as it sails into the roost.

The last of daylight was glimmering between serrated clouds as the main body of homecoming cranes sideslipped to shed altitude and cupped broad wings to reduce speed prior to landing. Descending in an upright standing position, they parachuted down western horizons bathed in fluorescent pink, red and chrome yellow transitions of light, long necks arched upwards, long black-fingered wings set, long legs dangling, long toes straining to touch the ground, before alighting daintily with a little run. The birds were still falling as darkness came and soon it was too dark to see them any more, although stragglers continued to arrive and call overhead.

Next morning I was already awake when first light touched the highlands; the crater, filled with fog, was a bowl of darkness. As the sun's rays slowly evaporated the mist, cranes were on the move, stalking stiff-legged up the western slope, then running a few steps, spreading their wings and flapping rapidly to get airborne before increasing speed with short hard upward flicks of their wingtips. I could hear their wings pumping and the slip of the wind in their feathers as they ascended.

The daily spectacle of the cranes' departures and returns to Bromfield Swamp would continue until the approach of the wet season, when stirrings of the mating urge would bear most of them aloft for the flight back to their nesting grounds in the Gulf Country.

The following day we drove north-west to the pretty central tablelands town of Atherton, the obvious base from which to explore nearby Hasties Swamp National Park. The Yidinji people know Hasties Swamp as Nyleta—'where the waters meet'—and though the tiny 57-hectare park is a mere remnant of the once extensive Nyleta Wetlands, it has only rarely dried out, ensuring its 224 recorded avian species a critical dry season refuge.

Sarus cranes, but not brolgas, are among the many birds that flock to Nyleta. Sarus have displaced brolgas in the wetter southern and central tablelands, including Nyleta, with brolgas now confined to strongholds in the drier northern and western areas. At the onset of the dry season the sarus migrate to Nyleta from wet season floodplains in the west to roost in its more permanent waters. Each day they return at dusk to their roost after spending the daylight hours feeding on farmlands.

Morning broke to fog on the day I visited, shrouding Nyleta in an alchemical glow, opaque and yet transparent. Weightless white mist hanging over the water and between the silhouettes of riparian trees caused shapes to dematerialise and contours to dissolve.

All around me leaves trembled in the mist, with droplets of water trapped at their tips. In these uplands, moisture in fog and clouds is captured on leaves or trunks and stored. Research has shown that this process, called 'cloud stripping' or 'cloud harvesting' can add as much as 40 per cent more water to total rainfall figures, increasing by billions of litres the flow to river systems and providing crucial moisture to high-altitude wildlife during the dry season.

A bird crossing the silver-and-grey-toned scene appeared as evanescent as a dream. Its passage and the squeal of a swamphen and the muffled flapping of wings against water were the only signs of the waking feathered life within.

Then, with the cool dawn, restless birds began to move in flurries. A big flock of plumed whistling ducks got up in a great slow easy flush and winged down-stream a hundred metres, where they settled again in long skating skids that raised patches of white water. Hard wings beating the air, a throng of cotton pygmy-geese passed with dazzling speed low over the water; wheeling in unison, their bellies flashed as silver as a shoal of darting herring. Gusts of small birds—red-browed finches and chestnut-breasted mannikins—blew down to the water's edge for a drink. Sarus cranes took heavy flight, peeling off to the north with unified grace, then climbing until distance erased them from sight and all that remained was the two-note horn blast of their voices drifting thin and clear across the marsh.

The eerie and beautiful voice of the sarus crane and brolga is broadcast via an elongated trachea, coiled like a French horn, that fills most of the anterior half of the birds' sternum. The trachea's rings fuse with the sternum to create thin plates that vibrate and amplify calls, which the cranes' Latin name *grues* is thought to imitate. Since the time of the vast marshes of the old ages, wherever it has resounded, that ancient bugle has evoked strong emotions in the people who heard it. It was a sound I wouldn't be hearing again until I had travelled far west of here, into a parched desert as different from this green and pleasant land as could be imagined.

After drinking, a red-browed finch bathes at Hasties Swamp. Seldom far from water, these eye-catching little birds form exuberant flocks outside the breeding season, producing swirling displays of colour.

CHAPTER SIX

Desert Brolgas

Out West where the stars are brightest, Where the scorching north wind blows, And the bones of the dead gleam whitest, And the sun on a desert glows—

—HENRY LAWSON, 'THE GREAT GREY PLAIN', 1893

This desert-adapted sand goanna obtains all its moisture from its food. Here it is digging in pursuit of a scorpion.

PAGES 90–1: *A pair of brolgas at rest in the vast and dehydrated Tirari Desert.*

On the face of it, Australia's forbidding central desert seems a strange place to seek a bird like the brolga that is most usually associated with wetlands. Whoever has visited Australia's mysterious heart knows that it is one of the driest places on Earth. Yet curiously, despite the infrequency and unpredictability of rain, these deserts harbour an astonishing diversity of water and shore birds. Practically all of them, including desert brolgas, have developed physiological and/or behavioural adaptations to Australia's extreme climatic variations, especially its capricious rainfall patterns.

Ecologically, brolgas are the most opportunistic of the world's fifteen species of cranes and the most variable in terms of habitat selection. In the arid zone, brolgas are traditionally dedicated wanderers, forever following the water, for even in dry times there is always some water somewhere.

Though Australia's deserts are harsh, they are also capable of the most startling abundance. They may look bare but they are not barren. After good inland rains, brolgas even penetrate the unforgiving Simpson Desert when claypans in sand dune swales multiply the region's temporary waterbird habitat. Pairs are also seen along the few river systems and on alluvial plains recently uncovered by receding floods. But the brolgas I was particularly interested in were those that have come to rely on one of the most profound changes European settlement has made to the outback ecology—artificial sources of permanent water.

Meeting up with these little-known cranes of the desert meant undertaking a very long road trip. After dropping off Steve Nott at Cairns Airport for his flight home, I drove due west, roughly following the course taken by brolgas and sarus cranes after they depart their dry season refuges on the Atherton Tableland and return to their wet season strongholds adjoining the Gulf of Carpentaria. On reaching the sleepy Gulf town of Normanton I turned south down the Burke Development Road, into the colossal emptiness of Queensland's flat and nearly featureless western plains, where the occasional butte and mesa such as Bang Bang Jump-up came into view long before I reached it.

A wedge-tailed eagle scavenges from a red kangaroo carcass.

The pink-eared duck is a dedicated desert wanderer.

OPPOSITE: *Stock watering points have encouraged an increase in desert dingo and galah populations.*

Stopping only to eat and sleep, I continued south through the isolated and thinly populated Channel Country in Queensland's south-western corner. With an average annual rainfall of less than 250 millimetres—too little to support crops—this is technically desert country. However, although arid in terms of the amount of rain that falls, the Channel Country's inhospitality is offset by the lacework of floodplain channels and braided streams, lined with corridors of tall river red gums and understorey vegetation, that give it its name. Flowing from the western slopes of the Great Dividing Range on average every three to five years, these waterways create refuges and paths along which birds, mammals and fish can migrate. At such times the Channel Country supports a great abundance of plants and animals when compared with deserts on other continents.

This fickle wealth of food sets in motion a great wave of life, drawing in brolgas and other nomadic birds from halfway across the continent. The ability of birds to reach resources quickly after they become available makes them far more successful in Australia—with its very large size, erratic climate and poor resource base—when compared with the continent's mammals. The number of Australian bird species, calculated on an area basis, is equivalent to or richer than that found on other continents, while its mammal fauna is very small when viewed on the same basis.

After a succession of good seasons, generations of the Channel Country's smaller animals radiate widely from their refuges over what would normally be parched regions. In the earth-cracking droughts that inevitably follow, the fair-weather birds leave and most of the vegetation wilts and dies, causing population crashes in plant-eating and dependent carnivorous animals. Only a few small permanent water sources remain in favoured core areas, allowing remnant groups of animals to survive till the next time of plenty.

Beyond the Channel Country and 2000 kilometres after leaving Cairns, I at last reached the remote settlement of Birdsville at the northern end of the fabled 481-kilometre Birdsville Track. After a couple of days exercising cramped muscles and exploring my new surroundings, I planned to follow the track across the nearby state border and begin my search for desert brolgas in the notoriously difficult terrain of north-eastern South Australia's Lake Eyre Basin.

I would be travelling between the Simpson Desert to the west and the Sturt Stony Desert to the east. Both are grim places with fearsome reputations. Their seemingly

life-denying expanses have a burnt, demonic aspect; endless red reaches of windspun sand or burnished stone exposed to bleaching light and heat that pours from an incandescent sky. Even in the age of all-pervasive 4WD-tourism, this alien landscape has managed to avoid the gaze of the modern world. Its ruggedness conspires against the unprepared and travelling through it evokes the pioneering spirit.

'Ya gotta take care of yourself out there,' a leather-skinned stockman from a nearby cattle station advised me when we met in the Birdsville Pub, headquarters for the approximately 6000 racing and boozing enthusiasts that swell the little town's population of 100 during its quirky annual Race Weekend. 'No use just hoping she'll be right.' He regarded me with a thin gleam of humour in his eyes, then joined in my startled laugh with a dry raven-croak laugh of his own.

In the wake of good rains, Darling lilies carpet an alluvial floodplain in this arid zone.

I set out at first light the next morning, and almost immediately after leaving Birdsville and crossing the Diamantina River I became aware of the fierce nature of the place I was entering. I had arrived in late winter but already there was a sting to the sun that promised worse to come. In summer the heat is infernal. Temperatures can reach 50°C. At the other extreme, during the short three-month winter, night temperatures often fall below freezing. Signs of the constant assault of natural forces—sandblasting, eroding, freezing and scorching—were everywhere. Even rocks suffer; boulders lay split in half by the elements like watermelons sliced by a machete.

I continued south down the graded red clay track on the lookout for brolgas in a naked expanse as far removed from the big birds' usual watery haunts as seemed possible. My journey was taking me through the driest part of the driest continent in the world except for Antarctica. Just north of the ruined and abandoned old Mulka store, where the track intersects the junction of the Tirari Desert, the Strzelecki Desert and the Sturt Stony Desert, I arrived at an otherwise anonymous place that boasts the lowest recorded annual average rainfall in the nation—less than 100 millimetres.

Usually reliant on ephemeral inland swamps and rivers to find prey, the white-necked heron is quick to take advantage of a permanent ground tank installed by graziers to water livestock.

An inland dotterel tends its eggs on a cauterised claypan.

OPPOSITE: *Transformed by heavy rain, this normally bare red-rock gibber desert has attracted nomadic bustards to the sudden cornucopia of insects, seeds and fruit.*

But this is a land of extremes rather than averages. When it does rain in this all-or-nothing country, heavy showers unhampered by vegetation pour down in a curtain of white water with enough force to buff the pebbles in the soil. Many desert plants spring to life at this time when the desert is, briefly, not a desert. The dust-to-deluge phenomenon triggers their dormant seeds to germinate. Some of these ephemeral plants are able to fit their entire life cycle into four weeks, painting the normally desiccated plains and dunes in instantaneous colours as an uprising of wildflowers produces huge volumes of seeds as quickly as possible so some may survive until the next rains.

To understand the magnetic pull Australia's deserts exert on those who know them—and I have known them in good times and bad—you need to see them now, when the land is awash with water and new growth. Blossoms in bleak places always seem the most welcome of all; they transform the desert's normally sombre hues into a garden larger than a man's imagination. Then, just as quickly, the dry times return. The colour is sucked out of the land, although the sky seems unfeasibly blue.

Buffered against the desert's hostility by conveniences like airconditioning, I found myself powerfully drawn to this Daliesque world of extremes and contrasts. By now I had reached one of Lake Eyre Basin's most hostile hot spots, the Sturt Stony Desert, a forbidding gibber desert that has been shaped by the elemental forces of nature. Gibber is from a Dharug word meaning 'stone', and with its hard 'g' it has the ring of solidity befitting this vast and shadeless plain overlaid with an interlocking chainmail of shiny yellowish-red lumps of quartz. Carved by water and honed by the wind, the gibbers lie like an immense mosaic; each stone seems to have been specially positioned and is separated by fine sand from its neighbour.

All this wide country was once the bottom of a vanished inland sea, or great lake, that had supported a pink fire of thousands of flamingos along its prehistoric shoreline. For many years it was accepted that the lake-haunting flamingos that had colonised other parts of the world in a great evolutionary radiation never reached Australia. Then, fossil finds in 1961–62 showed that at least six species (in four genera) had thrived here for millions of years until relatively recent times when Aboriginal people were firmly established, before dying out. Their extinction was tied to the gradual failure of rainfall during the last ice age, when increasing aridity caused the great chain of inland lakes to dry up. It was also partly due to the lack of freshwater springs from which flamingos need to drink and perhaps because Australia had become too poor in nutrients to support the metabolic demands of flamingos, except where sodium was concentrated to toxic levels. Instead, their place was taken by two much smaller but similarly specialised endemics, the banded stilt and pink-eared duck, which also feed on aquatic invertebrates using extremely modified beaks as filters.

Some of Australia's desert-adapted waterbirds, such as freckled ducks, banded stilts, and red-kneed and inland dotterels, are descended from early Gondwanan populations that survived after Australia's inland lakes evaporated. I was keen to take a closer look at one of them, the inland dotterel—a type of plover that, extraordinarily for a member of a family generally found along seashores and other bodies of water, has forsaken aquatic life altogether and lives mainly in the burning stony desert.

I set out on foot to look for it under a cloudless blue sky as sharp as sapphires. Not only is hiking the best way to learn wild country but it also presents the best chance of sighting a dotterel before this master of camouflage can meld into its background. When feeling threatened, inland dotterels crouch motionless with their cryptic dark-flecked buff backs turned to the intruder and become invisible against the amorphous rockscape. If caught resting in the shade of shrubs, they turn face-on, their disruptive black Y-shaped breast collar merging with the plants' stems.

A nagging wind blew out of the south. On the western horizon low buttes and mesas, called jump-ups or breakaways, rose like shadows into the wind, which rustled the primaries of a nankeen kestrel hanging in the air, fantailed and hovering. A little crow kept me under surveillance, its pale gaze fixed upon the trespasser. Calling derisively, it reminded me that, just because I'm human, I'm not so special.

I relished the long walk. Sometimes the most seductive landscapes are those most inimical to human life. Instead of scenic grandeur, these hard skylines manifested a fierce beauty and the timelessness of great solitudes. Deserts have always had a way of reinforcing the grip wild country has on the imagination, filling it with fear and longing, with equal amounts of yearning and trepidation. I was drawn to the paradox, the desert's alternate sublimity and ferocity, its blend of denial and subtle beauty; its mystical face, lovely and deadly.

In the late afternoon I finally came upon a pair of inland dotterels attending their winter nest, a sticks-and-stones-lined scrape in the flat bed of a claypan. The incubating parent was unhappy to see me and anxiously kicked a concealing cover of loose sand over three brown eggs before hurrying away with quick strides.

Taking a circuitous route back, my attention was attracted by two distant objects on the far side of the dry pan. Through binoculars, I was astonished to see a pair of brolgas standing nonchalantly on the bare mudflats adjoining the pan's scalded clay floor, beyond which encircling gibber downs extended to every distance. In that great emptiness, other than the brolgas, there was

A western grey kangaroo and her joey make the most of fields of salt-tolerant shrubs that have erupted after good rains. This brief burst of plenty will promote opportunistic breeding among kangaroos to compensate for the long lean years. Populations build up quickly and spread out in the good times, and contract and retreat to refuges in the bad.

*A haven for waterbirds, Mungerannie boredrain swamp was drilled in
1900 and, though now controlled, still flows along Derwent Creek for about
4 kilometres. Unlike the arid zone's typically ephemeral natural wetlands,
artificial water sources such as Mungerannie tend to be permanent, offering
critical refuge for waterbirds and birds that must drink.*

no sign of life. What had drawn these ethereal creatures to this denuded, cauterised place? Surely there was nothing for them here.

As it turned out, there was—as I later learnt from CSIRO field biologist Julian Reid, who first instructed me in the ways of the desert brolga. 'They were very likely foraging along the edges of the pan,' he suggested, 'looking for the roots of sedges and rushes buried in the cracking clay.'

On these arid plains, any depression in the Earth's surface exists only to hold water. Rain run-off cascading from the impervious gibber pavement drains into depressions called gilgais, and while usually they hold water for only short periods, falls of as little as 10 milli-metres can be enough to cover their entire bed with vegetation. Brolgas are especially attracted to large depressions that develop into ephemeral swamps, where tuberous sedges grow. The plants' underground corms, similar to a water chestnut, are rich in carbohydrate and a brolga staple.

'Brolgas concentrate on food items that are in abundance,' Julian told me. 'They'll return to a wetland even after surface water has evaporated, using their long stabbing bills to dig for corms and tubers in the dry bed until the local supply is exhausted.' By excavating so many conical holes brolgas will often leave a big piece of floodplain heavily pockmarked.

Brolgas are such an integral part of their austere habitat that it's been theorised they play a vital, albeit unknowing, role in the dispersal of certain invertebrate and plant species between isolated mound springs. Bubbling to the surface along the outer rim of the Great Artesian Basin—the world's biggest artesian ground-water basin, it underlies 1.7 million square kilometres of central and north-eastern Australia—these springs form an arc to the south and west of Lake Eyre.

One of the many conundrums confronting John Read—author of *Red Sand Green Heart*—during his nine years as ecologist at the Olympic Dam copper–uranium mine in northern South Australia, was the intriguing case of two species of tiny, poppy seed-sized hydrobiid snails and a rare plant, *Eriocaulon carsonii*. John found all three at mound springs that had not previously supported them. The question was: how did they get there, given that tracts of waterless desert separated them from the nearest source spring?

Based on the evidence, Dr Read was able to rule out the possibility that they had been washed down by floodwaters or carried on the hooves of horses or cattle. Nor was it probable that humans had deliberately or unintentionally transported them. 'The most likely vectors for dispersal were birds,' the lateral-thinking scientist concluded. 'Birds can fly long distances relatively quickly, thus enabling aquatic organisms to relocate while minimising the chances of desiccation.'

The best contenders to fill the conveyancing role were birds such as brolgas, herons, egrets, ibis and rails that forage in wetland vegetation. Brolgas were particularly likely candidates as they dislodge small fauna and flora while digging as deep as 15 centimetres into the mud on spring beds in search of food. Moreover, their big feet are well suited to carrying any miniature life forms they may disturb.

If, indeed, they are airlifting new life from one

mound spring to another, brolgas are playing an important role in the function of mound spring ecosystems. In that sense, they're much like the storks in the old folktale that bring new babies. Perhaps, John Read suggests, tongue-in-cheek, these cranes of the desert should more properly be known as the storks of the mound springs.

With their many endemic species, mound springs are extraordinary oases. They are formed by ancient water that comes to the surface from the subterranean lakes of the Great Artesian Basin, or GAB as it is popularly known. This underground water originated as rain falling mainly along the western slopes of Queensland's Great Dividing Range, with some recharge from the north-west. Moving at between 1–5 metres a year, it seeps into the basin through layers of porous rock on a journey that may take 2 million years. Some of it gushes out as springs, but since its discovery by Europeans in the early 1880s most of the artesian water that reaches the surface does so by artificial means.

Starting in 1883, bores were drilled into the GAB's hidden reservoir to provide water for communities and livestock. Their gradual increase between 1886–1914 created permanent artificially watered country. Ultimately, more than 23,000 bores were sunk right across the basin. With the bores came hundreds of kilometres of open channels, dug to deliver stock water. The biggest obstacle to squatting in this parched country had, it seemed, finally been overcome.

But new problems were in the making. Too many bores encouraged overstocking and pastures have been devastated. Falling internal pressure indicated that the aquifer itself was threatened. The fossil water is replenished only slowly. With many bores flowing uncontrolled, and with up to 95 per cent of water lost to evaporation and seepage, the original store has been depleted. The need to conserve water is recognised but many taps still flow free.

While it has become clear that the relatively straightforward action of installing a new water point results in a whole cascade of environmental effects that change the newly exposed areas, capping bores and installing poly-pipe to curb evaporation will also have profound environmental consequences. Many

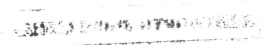

of the open channels, called boredrains, have developed into permanent wetlands. Some of these boredrain swamps have existed for over a century and function as artificial oases, providing prime habitat for the more than 170 bird species that have been recorded using them. Turning off the water benefits the aquifer but is detrimental to the birds that depend on it.

Practically all the brolgas in northern South Australia rely on these controversial sanctuaries to some extent and they were the brolgas I particularly wanted to take a look at. Driving south down the Birdsville Track, where over the decades a series of bores has been drilled at 40-kilometre intervals, I began to encounter the sand dunes of the Tirari Desert lapping up against the Sturt Stony Desert's gibber steppe. In that classic desert setting, the sudden appearance of pools of water bordered by tall bulrushes and lush sedges burst on the scene like a vision from the Old Testament.

This vivid slash of blue and green in an otherwise red and rusty yellow landscape announced Mungerannie boredrain swamp, a welcoming haven for humans and birds alike. Walking Derwent Creek, the natural drainage line that has received hot, pressurised artesian water from the borehead since 1900, I heard signals of life from everywhere around me. At first glance this hardly seemed like an artificial habitat, but even Mungerannie's bulrushes are imports, their fluffy seeds having wafted in on the wind.

Quietly 'talking' among themselves, a flock of apostlebirds drinks from and bathes in the overflow of a desert stock tank.

Bores like Mungerannie provide permanent potable water where there was none before, permitting pigeons, parrots and finches to colonise new country. Several species of waterbirds, such as crakes, rails and brolgas, have also been able to extend their ranges, as have reed- and sedge-frequenting birds such as reedwarblers, grassbirds and some chats. 'Most known brolga breeding in the Lake Eyre Basin has been in boredrain swamps,' environmental consultant Frank Badman, a 35-year veteran of these environs, told me. 'Brolgas and the rare yellow chat arrived from the river systems to the north.'

Wading birds are also big winners. Many native waders live at the bores throughout the year. Among the waders patrolling Mungerannie's still waters I noticed a migrant common sandpiper, south from Siberia. It was feeding in the company of other Palaearctic migrants—red-necked stints and a greenshank. Next month, in September, there would be many more arrivals fleeing the northern winter in favour of a globe-spanning endless summer.

Each austral spring a flood of nearly 2 million transient shorebirds—around 35 of the Northern Hemisphere's Arctic species—initiate three-week journeys of up to 10,000 kilometres from the northern parts of Russia, China and Japan to Australia. After reaching the mainland, many of them continue their incredible journey, following flyways across Australia's vast interior with pinpoint accuracy.

The large flocks of waders arriving from their northern breeding grounds are exhausted by the time they reach staging points like Mungerannie. The success of the trans-Australia leg of their migration depends on the welfare of chains of wetlands—coastal mudflats, lakes and swamps—across the continent, which serve as stopovers. Countless migratory birds perish en route each year and there is no way of knowing how many more would die were it not for the bores. After resting and building up their fat reserves, most of them fly on to coastal feeding grounds further south.

During his comprehensive ten-year survey of 177 boredrains in north-eastern South Australia, Dr Badman identified 22 as significant enough to warrant conservation. Those boredrains that provided the most important bird habitat also accounted for most of the water flowing from GAB bores. 'This was one case where bigger really is better,' he told me. 'I found that reducing water flow and thus the size of an artesian wetland has a direct influence on the number of bird species that inhabit it. A 50 per cent reduction in a boredrain's area may result in as much as a 90 per cent reduction in its productivity as bird habitat.'

While there is a general policy of closing down boredrains, the value of maintaining some, or certain parts of them—for social as well as environmental reasons—has been recognised by bodies like South Australia's Arid Areas Catchment Water Management Board. 'Some of these artificial wetlands provide an important focus for pastoralists and tourists, and help maintain local culture and lifestyles in an otherwise dry landscape,' the Board's Planning Officer, Ali Ben Kahn, told me.

A few hours' drive from Marree, the sunstruck little town at the southern end of the Birdsville Track, I stopped at Dulkaninna boredrain swamp to admire a sociable pair of brolgas stalking with long strides through open sedgelands. The sharp-eyed and alert birds were well aware of me but showed no fear. Because they have never been persecuted, the desert brolgas were the most trusting of all the cranes I encountered on my travels.

Watching them probe the mud for sedge tubers or occasionally chase after a grasshopper, it occurred to me that instead of the human-induced habitat losses of the past, we had for once wrought changes to the brolga's habitat that had helped secure their welfare. And, as is always the case with an umbrella species, the welfare of many other creatures that use boredrain swamps.

A pair of brolgas forages for sedge tubers as they wade ankle-deep in artesian water at Dulkaninna boredrain swamp. To reduce wastage and preserve water tables, the government is working with landholders to cap bores and replace open drains with pipelines. While laudable from a water economy point of view, such projects will disadvantage species, such as brolgas, that have become dependent on the water.

CHAPTER SEVEN

In the Riverina

Once there was no sun, only the moon and stars. Brolga and Dinewan the emu were quarrelling on a plain near the Murrumbidgee River. Brolga rushed to Dinewan's nest, seized one of her huge eggs and threw it into the sky. The yolk burst into flame and lit up the world below. A good spirit who lived in the sky decided to make a fire every day. He and his attendant spirits collect firewood and when the heap is big enough they send out the morning star to warn those on Earth that soon the fire will be lit.

—'HOW THE SUN WAS MADE', ABORIGINAL CREATION STORY

The Riverina takes its name from the Murray and Murrumbidgee rivers and their tributaries, and for those living there no single landmark is more central to the mythology of the region than the mighty Murray. History classes are devoted to retracing its early exploration, most notably Charles Sturt's trailblazing journey down this 'broad and noble river'. Six years later, Thomas Mitchell, Surveyor-General of New South Wales, followed the Lachlan and Murrumbidgee rivers to the Murray and on to the Darling River.

The Riverina has changed beyond recognition since Sturt traversed it in 1829–30. Much of what is now valuable cropland was originally an ancient riverine floodplain from which an estimated 15 billion trees were cleared and the land converted to agriculture and pasture. Realising the potential for irrigation, government authorities embarked on a series of public works projects that led to the construction of numerous locks, dams and weirs on the Murray and Murrumbidgee rivers in the 1920s and 1930s and would eventually turn the Riverina's Murray–Darling Basin into the nation's food bowl.[1]

I drove into this wide, rolling, sometimes hypnotic country on an early spring day that still retained a bracing hint of winter frost. Carrying personal invitations and precise directions on how to get where I was going, I headed for my first meeting with members of New South Wales' relict population of brolgas: birds so shy and so few and far between that not many people realise they still exist here. Before making their acquaintance, however, I wanted to get a sense of the changes to the landscape that have impacted not only brolgas and many other wild creatures but our own long-term wellbeing as well.

From the summit of Galore Hill—a looming 215-metre lone hump of rock in south-western New South Wales, roughly 45 kilometres by road from the state's largest inland city of Wagga Wagga—I gazed out over gold and green Riverina flatlands. Stands of flowering canola interspersed with cereal crops spread out in a steadily consolidating patchwork of fields. The epic prospect rolled away to the south, 50 kilometres down country,

Brolga expert Matthew Herring.

PAGE 108–9: *Viewed from the crest of Galore Hill, the Riverina spreads out in a steadily consolidating patchwork of green and gold farmlands.*

OPPOSITE: *A mated pair of brolgas exuberantly 'unison call' on a Riverina farm. This complex but carefully orchestrated duet helps form or reinforce pair bonds and also acts as a territorial warning to other nearby brolgas. During the display, the male elevates his wings over his back and initiates the antiphonal duet with a long series of low calls, which the female answers with two or three rapid high-pitched calls for each of his.*

visited here it had been in the grip of an El Niño-induced drought. There had been an overwhelming brownness to the look of the land, which had the threadbare texture of a worn brush.

In a region notorious for its highly variable climate, drought is a normal part of the meteorological history. Before the arrival of European settlers, the Riverina's landscape was an acutely sensed contradiction. That the Murray River could exist in this dry place, or all this dryness exist amid such water, seemed a conceptual disparity. But the river was merely passing through, sculpting a 2570-kilometre passage from its headwaters in the Snowy Mountains to its mouth at Encounter Bay, South Australia. This intricate and resilient ecosystem had evolved to survive droughts and, when floods came, to take quick advantage of conditions that favoured new life.

The re-engineering of the rivers undid 60, perhaps 70 million years of delicate natural plumbing. The Murray River that Sturt and Mitchell encountered was a pristine, untamed life force where Murray cod rooted in the shade of river red gums and black box crowding the water's edge. Sturt's eight-man crew caught so many cod they grew tired of eating them. Australia's largest true freshwater fish, it would become a potent symbol of the river, back when the Murray was a fisherman's paradise. Stories are told, and grainy old black-and-white photographs attest to the occasional catch that tipped the scales at 100 kilograms. But in the late 1990s, a comprehensive two-year freshwater survey did not catch or observe a single Murray cod in its namesake river system. 'Their population is highly fragmented,'

through broken light and shadow and distant storms that moved slowly along the horizon with their long dark tendrils trailing rain.

Earlier rains had ripened all the country around. Dam levels and farmers' spirits were equally high. The smell of recent rain on the vegetation gave a humid richness to the air that was almost sweet. The air itself was more appealing, with all those negative ions and raindrops scouring the atmosphere of dust particles. In the pretty little Lockhart Shire scenic reserve where I relaxed on a broad flat rock furred with yellow lichen, wildflowers were in brilliant colour.

The impact of colour and verdure was heightened by the contrast that had gone before it. The last time I had

Sprouting their first set of adult feathers, which will soon replace their fluffy down, these three-week-old rainbow lorikeet chicks will leave the nest in four to five weeks. Until then, they will be fed by both parents, who store partially digested food in their throat pouches before regurgitating it into the mouths of their ever-hungry babies.

Cattle egrets—with orange-buff head plumes—and intermediate egrets—with lacy plumes on their back—share a nesting colony on a Murray River floodplain. Flooding triggers waterbird breeding cycles so flood reduction due to river regulation has dramatically reduced breeding opportunities.

concluded the study's architect, New South Wales Fisheries scientist Dr John Harris, and largely restricted to 'key remnant areas'. In all, the study confirmed the threatened status of eleven species of native fish.

The once-mighty river of legend and pioneer lore was not just harnessed, it was turned into a series of placid pools. By the 1980s, with 90 per cent of their annual flow committed to agriculture, industry or water supply, the rivers of the Murray–Darling Basin were suffering severe environmental stress. Because of water extraction, the rivers now experience

drought level flows three out of every four years compared with one in twenty years in their naturally flowing state. Fish and birds lost critical breeding grounds when wetlands created by periodic flooding lost their water to the Hume Dam.

Once one of Australia's greatest waterbird rookeries, water regulation has had disastrous consequences for the Murray–Darling Basin. Despite their mobility, waterbirds have declined in many core wetlands now that they have fewer places to feed and breed. Richard Kingsford, wetland ecologist and principal research scientist for the New South Wales National Parks and Wildlife Service, recently released a paper reviewing the ecological impact of dams on floodplain wetlands. Every year since 1982, he and his colleagues have surveyed nearly 2000 wetlands across four states comprising almost half the continent. Between 1982 and 1990, following one of the worst droughts in the nation's history, the team averaged 850,000 waterbirds each survey. In the 1990s the average fell to 400,000. Now it's half that. The birds haven't gone elsewhere. They no longer exist.

Dr Kingsford and his fellow researchers have also been mapping the approximately 30,000 wetlands in the Murray–Darling Basin. It has become clear, he says, that the major river systems 'do not have many wetlands on them any more. Wherever we have looked, we are getting 50 per cent-plus loss of wetlands.'

In the nineteenth century, out of a belief that bogs were wastelands, Europe lost its wetlands to the plough and shovel. Driven by a parallel impulse, around half of south-eastern Australia's original shallow wetlands have been surrendered for pastures and crops. Such rapid and profound changes to the environment have reduced useable wildlife habitat to dangerous levels. Habitat specialists, as well as ground-nesting and ground-feeding birds, are especially at risk.

Habitat fragmentation, degradation and subsequent loss often pave the road to extinction. New evidence indicates that many of Australia's bird populations are showing signs of habitat-related stress and points to major long-term declines. A recent review by researchers Stephen Garnett and

A common brushtail possum peers from a Riverina eucalypt. The increasingly uncommon brushtail has largely vanished from central Australia, Cape York and the east coast, west of the divide. One reason may be competition with livestock for sparse resources during dry times when tree leaves become too desiccated for possums to eat and they must come down to feed on understorey plants. Predation by foxes is also to blame.

Gabriel Crowley listed nearly one-fifth of the continent's 1375 bird taxa (species, subspecies and races) as near threatened, threatened or extinct.

In New South Wales, the decline of the brolga was tied in fatal lock-step to agricultural development and the attendant staggering loss of freshwater wetlands through drainage, river regulation and 'improvement', water-storage construction, flood mitigation and the in-filling called land reclamation. A large part of the solution to this crisis—cutting water allocations to irrigators and delivering that water to the environment—was never going to be easy. Irrigators and conservationists agree the health of the rivers must be restored but they vociferously disagree over the timing and extent, and even the urgency of the reforms needed.

The Murray–Darling's average natural flow is around 13,800 gigalitres (gL),[2] of which over 11,000 gL are siphoned annually from the system. The federal government's National Water Initiative, a $500 million buyback that will return 500 gL to the Murray River, won't alleviate the problem. Freshwater ecologists believe 1500 gL a year is the minimum requirement.

The Murray–Darling and its wetlands can never be returned to their historical grandeur but a coordinated effort might achieve at least partial restoration. Rivers are remarkable that way. Provided they haven't been dammed out of existence, they resuscitate themselves at the slightest provocation, particularly compared with the slow recovery of terrestrial landscapes. But so far, despite a greater recognition of the problem, the long-term health of the Murray–Darling system has yet to be given a chance to recover by a significant increase in environmental flows.

The brolga's passing in New South Wales—if this must come—seems even more tragic given that in the colony's early days they were reputedly both common and remarkably trusting of humans. In 1839, naturalist and wildlife artist John Gould reported: 'I found it numerous in the neighbourhood of the Namoi and on the Brezi [sic] Plains … as well as on the low flat islands at the mouth of the Hunter. It is very easily tamed: when at Parramatta I saw a remarkably fine example walking about the streets in the midst of the inhabitants, perfectly at ease.'[3]

Once sufficiently abundant and widespread to be regarded as a pest to crops, beginning in the 1800s brolgas steadily vanished from many former New South Wales strongholds, including around Sydney. Those that persist are largely confined to north-east New South Wales, the Moree, Walgett, Bourke, Wanaaring and Milparinka areas, the Riverina wetlands and the Macquarie Marshes.

Past shooting and poisoning campaigns by some farmers, who resented brolgas for consuming grain seeds and damaging the shoots of new green crops, exacerbated the die-off. Although by then illegal, as recently as 1970 at least 300 brolgas were shot in one day during an organised drive on Lake Urana, south-west of Wagga Wagga. Though nobody in New South Wales hunts them any more, any recovery in brolga numbers has been inhibited by the predation of young birds by a burgeoning population of European red foxes.

Once a leafy stand of riverine woodland on the Murray River floodplain, this graveyard of drowned trees is a by-product of a dam that transformed land into water. River regulation has also adversely affected the riparian environment by reducing the frequency of the flooding that red gum forests depend on for germination.

Brolga parents share incubation duties, exchanging roles every couple of hours during the day. The new incubating parent turns the eggs with its bill (right) in order to prevent adhesions between the membranes and to warm them equally on both sides. During the first month after hatching, the chick's legs grow rapidly (above) and it looks ungainly, with no hint of the elegant adult to come. Wing development proceeds more slowly but speeds up as the young approach fledging, at about fourteen weeks.

As the southern brolgas' range dwindled—and because central New South Wales is almost devoid of brolgas—this small sub-population has become largely isolated from the large flocks of northern Australia. A shrinking population risks losing genetic variation through inbreeding, resulting in lowered levels of fitness and reproduction. During the breeding season bonded brolga pairs are highly territorial, zealously guarding and defending nest sites, thus the south's loss of suitable breeding habitat could mean inbreeding is increasing as each year the same pairs produce young. So, though at the national level brolgas are neither rare nor endangered, in New South Wales, Victoria and South Australia, their tentative clawhold on survival has seen them classified as a threatened species.[4]

'We know that in total there are fewer than 1000 brolgas scattered across the far south-east of South Australia, south-western Victoria and the New South Wales and Victorian Riverina,' conservation biologist and brolga specialist Matthew Herring told me when I earlier stopped by his Albury home base on the upper Murray River. For a bird of its size, stately appearance and striking social behaviour, surprisingly little was known about the brolgas of New South Wales before Matt's timely study. Tall, outgoing and filled with a youthful enthusiasm for life, this ardent-hearted young man has for six years researched the Riverina brolgas—focusing on their distribution, breeding habitat and role as an umbrella species—for his Honours thesis with Charles Sturt University.

Matt has come to the unhappy conclusion that the damage done to the Riverina's natural resources is so irrevocable that much of it is beyond remedy. 'Now it's the quality and management of both remnant and constructed wetland habitat that's of greatest importance,' he believes. 'Our best hope involves incorporating large-scale approaches, rural communities and private land to break the vicious downward spiral of renewable resource degradation.'

Rather than abandon the Riverina's last brolgas to whim and neglect, to be exterminated in the name of inevitability, Matt has actively promoted community participation in brolga research and conservation. He knows that conservation campaigns that stand the greatest chance of being accepted by the rural community are those that forge partnerships between government, private landholders and conservationists. 'Community involvement helps increase awareness,' he says, 'and can lead to private conservation projects.' That's important for a species that relies heavily on privately owned wetlands, particularly in the Riverina where less than 1 per cent of the landscape is in conservation reserves.

With the help of mass media and via word of mouth, Matt established a volunteer community-based observer network to assist in his research. The 220 mostly private landholders—which through their own initiative mushroomed to involve close to 1000 observers—were invaluable in helping him to obtain brolga distribution and abundance records and locate breeding and flocking sites in his study area. 'Landholders are very attached to the brolgas on their properties,' he discovered. 'A lot of them I've spoken to are quite concerned that the brolgas their grandparents were so used to seeing mightn't be around for their own grandchildren.'

I was on my way to the stud farm of one of those landholders where, at a secret location, a pair of brolgas was known to be nesting. Blowing clouds, like grey rags, chased across the sky as I drove, splitting the sun into rays that splayed in different directions. Fitful spits of rain sputtered on the roof of my vehicle.

Several months earlier the onset of winter rainfall had initiated a chain of events for the brolgas of the Riverina that was now culminating in the hatching of young. As the storms blow in, the brolgas become restless. Calling and circling, they at last depart the more permanent communal flocking wetlands at Urana–Jerilderie, Barooga, Corop–Stanhope, Dingee–Pyramid Hill and Tuckerbil Swamp near Leeton, and set course for isolated, ephemeral breeding wetlands scattered throughout the Riverina. Here they live in solitary pairs while breeding between July and December, each as far as defended territories permit from the next pair. They celebrate their return with exuberant leaps, wing flapping and loud trumpet duets— fervent courtship displays that stimulate hormonal changes in the female's body which advance ovulation and the desire to mate.

According to brolga expert Gavin Blackman, male brolgas don't breed until their fourth or fifth year while most females begin breeding when three years old. Sub-adults usually associate with several potential mates before a firm bond is established. Whereas established pairs mate with facility and a lack of tension, new pairs engage in long bouts of dancing before attempting copulation. Their first breeding attempt—and, quite often, their second—is apt to fail, and pair bonds are not considered permanent until they have reproduced. Folklore aside, brolgas do not mate for life unless reproduction is relatively successful. Established pairs,

SEASONAL CYCLE OF THE BROLGA IN SOUTH-EAST AUSTRALIA[5]

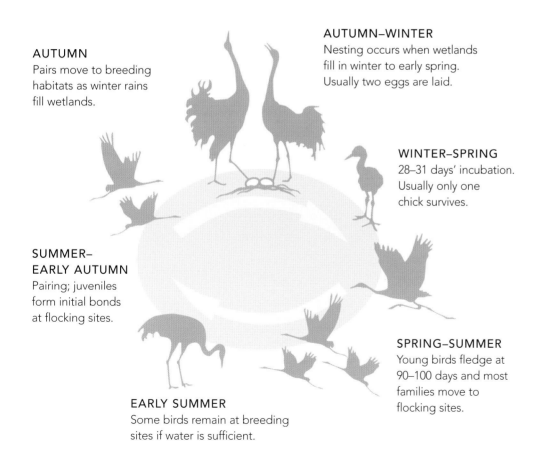

AUTUMN
Pairs move to breeding habitats as winter rains fill wetlands.

AUTUMN–WINTER
Nesting occurs when wetlands fill in winter to early spring. Usually two eggs are laid.

WINTER–SPRING
28–31 days' incubation. Usually only one chick survives.

SUMMER–EARLY AUTUMN
Pairing; juveniles form initial bonds at flocking sites.

SPRING–SUMMER
Young birds fledge at 90–100 days and most families move to flocking sites.

EARLY SUMMER
Some birds remain at breeding sites if water is sufficient.

however, remain monogamous until one partner dies, breeding annually for at least fifteen years in the wild and a good half-century in captivity.

Mated pairs select breeding territories that offer food, nest sites and areas of dense cover that can conceal the young when danger threatens. During his investigation into brolga breeding habitat, Matthew Herring visited all 32 breeding sites in his study area and compared them with 27 non-breeding sites and 35 randomly selected wetland control sites in order to identify important selection criteria.

He found that most pairs preferred to nest in or on the edge of large (30–200 hectare), ephemeral, well-vegetated freshwater marshes or wet meadows. Over 90 per cent of breeding sites were dominated by cane grass or spike rushes and were situated in extensive areas of water around 30 centimetres deep, with little or no tree cover and panoramic all-round views. Deeper marshes, brackish wetlands, lakes and farm dams were less frequently used, while nesting on dry land was rare.

'Many wetlands of the type preferred by breeding brolgas have been lost since European settlement,' Matt told me. 'A lot of swamps identified on old maps simply don't exist any more.' The management of flooding, grazing and fire regimes at the remaining breeding sites is critical, he says, as these three elements have a huge impact on the structure and composition of wetland vegetation. 'For instance, cane grass and cumbungi [bulrushes] can form thick rank stands over 2 metres tall. Nesting brolgas need to keep a wary eye out for predators and so avoid sites with tall

robust waterplants.' Striking a balance between too much wetland plant cover and not enough is at the heart of this challenge. Fortunately for brolgas, cane grass and cumbungi are sometimes burnt or crash-grazed to encourage succulent shoots for livestock.

Matt had earlier made arrangements with the owners of a property in the Urana district for me to photograph a pair of brolgas nesting on an ephemeral freshwater meadow not far from their farmhouse. Most landowners are very protective of *their* brolgas and I had to promise that in no way would I disturb them. As it turned out, nesting so close to the house meant that this pair had learnt to tolerate humans with remarkable equanimity. As long as I moved slowly and didn't get too close, they went about their affairs as if I wasn't there.

The nest site had been used previously, probably because birds return to nest where they have had past success—one pair was recorded using the same site for twenty years. Like all cranes, this male and female shared nest-building, incubation and chick-rearing.

Nest construction, which takes from one to seven days, began with the two of them pulling up nesting material—mainly sedge stems, uprooted grasses and other plants—and tossing it backwards over their shoulders. The accumulated material was then gathered and heaped into a massive raised mound about 1.5 metres in diameter. So many nearby plants had been collected that a 'moat' had formed around the nest. Hopefully it would provide some protection from terrestrial egg-thieves.

Soon after finishing the nest, the first egg was laid.

The golden light of early morning reflects a purple swamphen in the clear water of a pristine marshland. More than 90 native waterbird species have been recorded in the Murray–Darling Basin, but their wellbeing is dependent on suitable wetlands for both feeding and breeding. As waterbirds require clean water they are sensitive indicators of the biological health of their ecosystem.

I arrived two days later just as the clutch was completed with the arrival of a second ovule-pointed cream-coloured egg, decorated with reddish-brown and lavender specks of pigment. Brolgas, like other crane species inhabiting warmer parts of the world, produce light-coloured eggs that reflect heat while cranes in colder climates lay darker, heat-absorbing eggs.

Once the eggs were laid, the pair exchanged incubating responsibilities about every two hours. During the changeover they bugled wild unison calls, reinforcing the pair bond and again proclaiming dominance over their

nesting territory. Then the off-duty bird would usually fly some distance to a favourite feeding area. At night they both stayed near the nest, the female doing most of the incubation while the male stood guard.

Incubation lasted for around 30 days and then within 24 hours of each other the downy silver-grey chicks 'pipped' their way to freedom with a well-developed egg tooth that they would lose a few days later. High-pitched peeps announced the 100-gram hatchlings' breakout and their parents answered with low purring contact calls. A day later the chicks developed a soft food-begging peep to which the adults responded with offerings of insects and spiders. Hatching coincides with the emergence of insects that parents feed to the young until their bills develop sufficiently to probe for their own prey.

The chicks' rate of growth was phenomenal—up to 25 millimetres per day. Their long legs grew particularly rapidly during the first six weeks and walking strengthened their joints. Soon they could run and keep up with the long-striding adults as they foraged. Chicks can also swim for the first two to three weeks of their lives, after which they either can't or won't swim.

Within a day of hatching the newly mobile chicks were led from the telltale nest into the shelter of the marshland's emergent vegetation. Though the parents removed all broken shells—some bits were discarded, others consumed by the female, perhaps to replace calcium used by her body to coat the eggs—the inevitable commotion caused by the hatchlings might have alerted a sharp-eyed predator.

In the competition for food one chick invariably dominates; the weaker of the two, stressed and starved, succumbs quickly. For the remaining chick the first three weeks after hatching are the most dangerous; many perish within the fourteen weeks before they can fly, the great majority apparently from predation.

Predation by raptors such as swamp harriers and whistling kites, and by ravens, crows, goannas, eels, water rats, feral cats, even purple swamphens, is a constant threat to flightless brolga chicks, but in southern Australia they are particularly vulnerable to the fox's slashing incisors. Matt Herring's

Healthy freshwater wetlands such as this carry dozens of species of native aquatic plants, including the delicate fringed petals of the yellow-flowering wavy marshwort. Half of south-east Australia's original shallow wetlands have been drained but, encouragingly, a partnership between Riverina conservationists, landholders and government has embarked on a range of promising wetland restoration projects.

study revealed that only 30 per cent of nesting attempts succeed. Such a low reproductive rate inevitably slows recovery from population losses.

Brolga breeding success can be difficult to determine, especially post-fledging survival, but Matt found the easiest way to measure recruitment was by counting the number of immature birds in the flocks at each of the five main summer flocking sites in his study area. Chicks are fully feathered at 80–90 days and fledge about ten days later. Those that survive the dangerous first year remain with their parents for up to eleven months until the onset of the next breeding season or almost two years if the adults do not re-nest. Though juveniles attain full adult size in their first summer, their bills are brownish and until they are 22 months old they lack the distinctive red caruncle (or comb) that ornaments the rear of an adult's naked grey-green crown. The pale orange skin on a juvenile's feather-covered head is relatively easy to distinguish.

Matt discovered that, alarmingly, recruitment after a good one-in-four-year season was an unsustainable 4.4 per cent—one-quarter of the northern brolgas' replacement rate, where up to 17 per cent is commonplace. It has become apparent that, unless something is done, the threat posed by lack of habitat and a high fox density is pushing the last of the southern brolgas to the edge of extinction.

Their only hope of a comeback at this late stage depends on the species that got them into trouble in the first place. 'There's now a great deal of wetland conservation targeted at brolgas in south-eastern

Australia,' Matt pointed out with pragmatic optimism. He listed a promising range of restoration projects currently under way. 'Many farmers are beginning to turn things around by applying for environmental water flows. They flood depressions on their properties that have become isolated from the floodplains by using the irrigation infrastructure. They also avoid grazing wetlands when they are full and have bumped up their fox control efforts.'

Brolgas will breed in the right kind of small artificial wetlands, so landholders with large storage or recycling dams are in an ideal position to establish breeding habitat. Matt has worked on several constructed wetland projects where modifications to existing sites or the creation of entirely new wetlands have clearly benefited brolgas, other threatened waterbirds and biodiversity generally. Establishing earthworks to create seasonally flooded shallows about 30 centimetres deep with a good cover of emergent waterplants is one very successful technique. Predator-proof fencing is being trialled to improve breeding success by keeping foxes out. Hopefully the new wetlands will become outdoor Petri dishes from which the seeds of restoration will come.

The beginning of the new millennium seemed a compelling time to take a close look at the often-fraught relationship between wild animals and humans. From the moment a person first set foot on an Australian shore 50,000 years ago our species has played an active role as direct agent of environmental change and the cause of the extinction of other species. Now we are down to our last options.

'In south-eastern Australia brolgas have become a flagship species for wetland biota and deservedly so,' Matt notes. 'Their breeding sites are particularly rich in bird life.' Baillon's and spotted crakes, glossy ibises, black swans, purple swamphens and red-kneed dotterels prosper at brolga sites, and one-third of those sites support the rare, cover-dependent Australasian bittern; a handful even boast the near-mythical Australian painted snipe.

'Biodiversity is about preserving entire ecosystems that prop everything up, and brolgas are sensitive indicators of the ecological health of their wetland habitat,' says Matt. 'Their recovery may mean hope for many other species.' It was a challenge I would further investigate as I proceeded south to western Victoria's volcanic plain.

CHAPTER EIGHT

Beneath the Grampians

Brolga and Emu were grinding grass seeds to eat. Emu became jealous of Brolga's grinding stone and swallowed it. Brolga whacked Emu on the back and he coughed up the stone. Emu got so angry that he hit Brolga on her head with a stick, which is how Brolga got her red cap.

—'HOW BROLGA GOT HER RED CAP', ABORIGINAL CREATION STORY

Yellow-tailed black cockatoos seeking cones in a copse of radiata pines behind my camp wailed harsh alarm calls on first noticing me but soon settled when I remained sitting quietly, watching the local life go by. To the south-east, shrouds of dull smoke—stubble burn-off prior to sowing—ascended to form an eerie rust-coloured fire cloud. Spectral sky-specks—silently drifting kites riding thermals on extended wings in pursuit of prey roused and panicked by the flames—circled the smoky heavens. Mottled-brown, tail-wagging Richard's pipits hotfooted it across the black fire-scorched earth on the lookout for broiled grasshoppers and beetles. On the north-western horizon, the Grampians—an irregular fence of grey and red-streaked saw-toothed sandstone mountains—rose like a 400 million-year-old exclamation mark on the southern tip of the Great Dividing Range.

It was April of the following year, and I was making the second of my two visits to John and Lynne Anderson's 720-hectare merino, wheat and canola farm on the volcanic plains of south-western Victoria's Willaura district. Like my first visit, in early December, this one was timed to coincide with the southern brolgas' flocking season, between late November and June. In accordance with traditions dating from ancient times, most pairs of brolgas depart their individual nesting territories after breeding and fly with their young of the season, if they have succeeded in raising any, to the same small number of post-breeding sites where they form loose non-territorial flocks.

The Andersons' farm, between the villages of Willaura and Glen-thompson, and the properties surrounding it, form one of the most important brolga flocking sites in Victoria, regularly attracting around 200 of south-western Victoria's estimated total population of 650–675 brolgas. It's a spectacular gathering of a species now only rarely seen in southern Australia.

I had been introduced to the Andersons by Rebecca Sheldon, a young University of Ballarat Honours student who was busy identifying existing brolga flocking sites and locating potential new ones using field surveys and a Geographic Information System (GIS). Because most flocking sites are on private land, she found herself working closely with local farmers who furnished her with crucial information she was more than generous in

A brolga's salt-encrusted feather lies on the bed of a drying saline lake in western Victoria.

PAGES 128–9: *Beneath the Grampians, brolgas glean harvest waste in a burnt stubble-field bordering the crystalline salt lake where they roost.*

OPPOSITE: *With a high flapping leap, a young unpaired male brolga in search of a mate begins an enthusiastic courtship dance. His display could lead to a casual attachment, which may or may not result in permanent pair bonding. Dancing is often contagious within flocks, spreading rapidly among the excited birds.*

granting me access to, along with her valuable time and research data.

We first met one cold wet winter's day when I joined her and Claire Harding, a friend and colleague, in the countryside near Skipton, west of Ballarat, to check on several active brolga nests they were monitoring. Claire had recently completed her Honours thesis on brolga breeding ecology in south-west Victoria, using Landsat satellite imagery to locate suitable brolga breeding habitat. Her work, it is hoped, will set in motion strategies to help boost the size of the south-west's brolga population, which census figures suggest has remained static for over two decades.

Though the population appears to be unchanging, little or no recruitment means that the community as a whole may be ageing. Brolgas are long-lived birds, with a lifespan of up to 40 years in the wild and 80 years in captivity, so a drop in their reproduction rate may go unnoticed until older birds begin dying, setting the stage for a sudden catastrophic population crash.

Claire's research indicates how many breeding pairs of brolgas the region can support and offers management strategies to landowners whose properties have potential breeding habitat on ways to improve brolga breeding success. With Victoria's remaining cranes facing daunting obstacles to rearing a chick—not the least of which is the loss of nearly 80 per cent of their preferred breeding habitat—it's a goal that invokes its own special brand of urgency.

As one of the first parts of the nation converted to agriculture, the Victorian volcanic plain has little public land and its few parks and conservation reserves are small and scattered. The creation of this almost entirely artificial environment was not achieved at one stroke, nor is it complete. With much of the district in private ownership, the future of its brolgas and the other 118 known threatened species of fauna and flora, not to mention the undetermined number of threatened ecological communities, depends largely on individual landowners. In the past, before habitat loss and fences, these plains were part of an immense natural regional flow of moisture, nutrients and wildlife.

'Travelled NE through one of the most magnificent arable and pasture countries in the world … kangaroo and emu running before us … quails, parrots and cockatoos,' exulted Captain Foster Fyans while

Without striking a wingbeat, the kites ride a thermal, silently circling on the lookout for insects, reptiles and small mammals fleeing the flames of a fire in the stubble-fields below.

surveying these gently undulating plains in 1839.[1] I could empathise with Fyans' delight as he contemplated the dramatic landscape: sweeping temperate grasslands dotted with patches of open woodland and punctuated with the low peaks of long-extinct volcanoes, some surrounded by stony rises denoting old lava flows. There were hundreds of lakes, many formed by a slumping of the lava crust. Countless peat swamps rose where valleys were dammed and streams blocked by primordial lava flows.

From the beginning, European explorers and settlers spoke of the watery nature of these fertile plains. While attempting to negotiate broad swamps on the way to the Grampians in 1836, Grenville Staplyton, assistant to Surveyor-General Thomas Mitchell, cursed: 'All bogged and bedevilled … damn

*The craggy sandstone escarpment at Boroka Lookout provides visitors to Grampians National
Park with a perfect perch from which to contemplate Lake Bellfield and the surrounding plains.
'A vast champagne country', wrote Chief Protector of the Aborigines, George Augustus
Robinson, while travelling south of the Grampians in 1841. 'Covered with thick and fine
grass … saw a great number of turkeys [bustards] on our way.'*

the bullock drivers, bullocks, drays, wagons and all.' In 1839, the surveyor C.J. Tyers 'discovered we were hemmed in on all sides by swamps and stony ridges'.

German squatter Wilhelm Habel noted in 1882 that Lake Linlithgow, just east of the regional centre of Hamilton, supported

myriads of ducks, hundreds of swan, [magpie] geese, plover, pelicans and, during the morning and evening, native companions [brolgas] in great numbers … During the last few weeks farmers in the Lake Lithgow [sic] district have been busily engaged in burning stubble and the fields are now the haunt of native companions and plover. These can be counted by the thousand and can easily be brought in range by the sportsman creeping up to the bank of the lake. As the much talked of turkeys [bustards] are conspicuous by their absence, and native companions, if properly bled, buried etc. are not bad eating, a profitable hour's sport can be obtained.[2]

If brolgas made not bad eating, the big imposing Australian bustard was admired as haute cuisine by Europeans. Captain Cook remarked: 'We all agreed that this was the best bird we had eaten since we left England.' Once found throughout Australia except for the denser forests of the east coast, bustards were formerly one of the commonest large birds in Victoria but are now extremely rare here. Uncontrolled shooting and habitat destruction have wiped them out from virtually the whole of south-eastern Australia.

Habitat destruction began with the first settlers. As early as 1862, one prescient western plains squatter, G.T. Lloyd, noted with alarm the rapid changes to the land brought about by the introduction of sheep. 'No sooner had the rich native pastures been well fed down and, as a consequence, every

A crackling roar and a column of smoke rising from a stubble-field attracts whistling kites (pictured on page 133) to a feast.

square inch of land continually impressed with the little hooves of sheep, than the whole of the occupied country began to assume a totally different aspect.'[3]

The soft, boggy terrain had, over aeons, evolved an immensely efficient system for trapping and storing water. Vegetation absorbed and kept moisture on the landscape in a vast mosaic of self-sustaining wetlands and grasslands. Groundwater was trapped between the clay subsoil just below the surface and loam topsoil that had never known a hoof before 1788. By 1860, however, the south-eastern corner of the continent carried 20 million sheep and 4 million cattle; 30 years later cattle numbers had doubled and sheep increased

In the highlands of the Great Dividing Range, a young wombat eases the autumn chill by basking atop an exposed boulder.

fivefold. Their hard hooves trampled the fragile soil to dust, tamping it down so hard that roots could not penetrate it or water sink into it.

Overcrowding livestock overwhelmed the highly evolved natural water system, causing the landscape to drain very quickly, the opposite of how it had been before European intervention. The whole texture of the place was different. 'Two years occupation in most instances rendered a station so "firm" that horse racing, kangaroo, emu and dingo hunting formed one of the principal sources of amusement to the light-hearted settlers,' Lloyd observed.

Dense herds of livestock soon overgrazed native perennial grasses and herbs. Succulent kangaroo grass (*Themeda australis*), 'waving like a crop', dominated the better-drained prairies. Lloyd cautioned that 'kangaroo grass, the most successful Australian herbage' needed careful management or it 'will soon be exterminated'. His warning went unheeded. The introduction of exotic grasses and clover plus superphosphate in the 1930s was the final step in the transformation. Of Victoria's original floristically rich native grassland complexes, today less than 1 per cent remains.

The discovery of alluvial gold in the 1850s accelerated the forces of change as people poured into the interior. When the gold ran out, unemployed diggers turned to the land and were joined by new settlers. Demands for pasture and agricultural land prompted the draining of swamps as one way to acquire rich soil. In western Victoria, 78 per cent of the shallow freshwater meadows and swamps were lost or extensively modified through drainage.

Quintessentially Australian, these ephemeral inland wetlands are biologically diverse and highly productive wildlife habitats. Many that survived drainage have progressively lost their original sedges, pond lilies, reeds, pencil rushes, water milfoil and water ribbons to grazing livestock that gained summer access when water levels fell. In the final phase of disruption, bare pools, white with crystalline salt or pink with algae, are replacing undamaged wetlands as the loss of water plant associations is accelerated by rising salinity—a by-product of 150 years of tree-felling and ringbarking.

The passage of the Land Act in 1884, requiring the clearing of trees to obtain freehold, resulted in the loss of almost all of the region's woodlands, and there is little regeneration of what remains due to grazing and cropping. Deep-rooted trees are thirsty drinkers and keep the watertable down. When they disappear a delicate balance is broken. Over time water begins to rise—often very salty water, a legacy on these plains that dates back 14 million years to a time when the ocean lapped the Grampians. These days, the insidious and intractable threat that is dryland salinity is the most pressing environmental problem facing the nation.

For wildlife, changing vegetation patterns ushered in the forlornly familiar cycle of decline and extirpation that accompanies pervasive habitat loss. Competition with domestic stock meant smaller marsupials like the eastern barred bandicoot and terrestrial birds like the plains-wanderer were eaten out of house and food supply. The great flocks of magpie geese had disappeared by the end of the nineteenth century, hunted for the table and the market, although the draining and grazing of their reedy marshlands was equally to blame. Any further reduction in the number of shallow swampy areas will lead to a further brolga population decline. Sometimes referred to as an 'indicator' species because their fortunes are so closely tied to the fate of their wetlands, brolgas are reliant on a diversity of lagoons, marshes and backwaters of rivers.

The brolga's habitat requirements are closely linked to its seasonal life cycle, which in turn is determined by rainfall patterns. Early each summer, with the drying of the shallow wetlands in their nesting territories, the brolgas of the southern Grampians return to their post-breeding flocking sites. Not all make the flight; some bonded pairs and their newly fledged young remain close to their nest site. But most depart. Some cross the border, headed for South Australia's Bool Lagoon. By responding to an innate urge to over-summer on a big freshwater swamp like Bool they are sticking closest to brolga tradition. Bool Lagoon and Willaura are both traditional flocking sites while five other areas at Strathdownie, Dundonnell, Streatham, Skipton and Cressy are used regularly by smaller flocks, as well as some other less frequently used sites.

Masked lapwing parents protectively shelter a newly hatched chick. The precocious chick will quit the scrape-in-the-ground nest within a few hours of hatching and be led away by the adults, who cooperate in brooding and vigorously defend their three to four young.

Most Victorian brolgas have adapted to the scarcity of large well-vegetated marshes like Bool Lagoon by congregating at permanent open pools and on adjacent farmlands. They arrive shortly after the autumn cereal grain crops—particularly wheat and the wheat/rye cross called triticale—have been threshed down to stubble and forage almost exclusively in the harvested fields. Indeed, these brolgas now follow agricultural cycles and not until the crops are headed do they return. As the supply of fallen grain declines, brolgas turn to grain fed to sheep and sown grain sprouting after the first good autumn–winter rains. This entails added expense to the birds' grain-growing hosts but they remain unstintingly generous towards their visitors.

During this six to eight months of their annual cycle, brolgas of both sexes

Brolgas flocking on a beef, wheat and canola farm at Penshurst in western Victoria share a natural freshwater roost with Australian shelducks and black swans. Creatures of tradition, young brolgas learn the best flocking and breeding places from their parents, generation by generation. Poor flocking sites are likely to be abandoned, while locations with safe roosts and ample food will host the same brolgas year after year, and attract others on the move.

Once common near watercourses on the grassy, eucalypt-dominated slopes of the Great Dividing Range, the diamond finch is now listed as near-threatened due to habitat destruction. This dapper little seed-eater is one of a suite of species that has declined as woodlands in south-east Australia have been felled. Even remaining habitat fragments are becoming unsuitable as invasive exotic grasses replace the diamond finch's key food plants.

and all ages gather at flocking sites. In contrast to solitary pairs' aggressively anti-social ways when nesting, flocking helps ease group tensions, although families remain self-contained and coordinate their activities with one another rather than with the flock as a whole.

There's not much time for social activity during intensive morning feeding, but in the afternoons long periods of 'loafing' permit a good deal of interaction. Established couples reinforce their pair bond by bill-fencing and dancing. Being spirited creatures, disputes occur, usually over a choice feeding spot, but are quickly settled. Establishing a hierarchy on flocking grounds is safer than on a nesting territory, where fights between residents and intruders can lead to injury or even death. When roosting together, however, etiquette requires that these feisty birds stand at least a peck distance away from their neighbour.

This seasonal gathering on neutral ground encourages another critical social function: unpaired young adults have the chance to meet prospective mates and perhaps form pair bonds before scattering for the breeding season. I sometimes saw inexperienced adolescent males, eager to experiment with a more complex social life, misdirect their dance displays towards females that were already paired or even towards other males. Their social gaffes always ended with the chagrined would-be suitor being chased off in no uncertain manner. Eventually a receptive female would reciprocate his display and a casual attachment form that could lead to permanent bonding.

In order to assess preferred flocking habitat, Rebecca Sheldon needed to map Victoria's flocking site distribution, past and present. Records showed that, apart from a small population of between 80–120 birds on the north-central riverine plains and adjacent parts of the Murray River, their current range has contracted to the volcanic plains of the Western District and the southern Wimmera. The latter area is bounded by Geelong in the east, Horsham and Ballarat in the north, Portland and Warrnambool in the south and the South Australia–Victoria border in the west. In former days brolgas also occurred across the coastal plains of east Gippsland and Port Phillip Bay. Small flocks were found on French Island in Western Port Bay until 1919 and on the plains and wetlands of the Sale area until the 1920s. They were once common in the Rutherglen area of north-eastern Victoria and so plentiful around Melbourne that they were sold as food in the Melbourne market. Nowadays, due to habitat loss, the Western District brolgas are isolated from those in northern Victoria and the Riverina.

To identify the ecological characteristics of brolga flocking habitat, Rebecca selected 29 wetland sites for analysis based on site fidelity, brolga abundance and flocking duration. Historically brolgas flocked mainly on deep freshwater marshes with shallow margins or permanent open pools—fresh and saline—greater than 30 hectares in size and with a cover of emergent vegetation. However, the salinisation of the region's waterways has resulted in many wetlands becoming hyper-saline. Though brolgas use salt marshes more than other cranes—they are the only cranes to have specialised glands near the eyes through which they are able to secrete concentrated salts—these despoiled ponds no longer support water plants or carry only a few tough, adaptable species. They are no substitute for the freshwater swamps where once brolgas dug for the roots of sedges and hunted frogs and large insects.

Rebecca Sheldon is the most recent in a succession of conservationists anxious to conserve Victoria's brolga flocking habitat. Her study continues a project started by the late Graham Pizzey, one of Australia's foremost ornithologists. Shortly before his death, Graham made an impassioned appeal on behalf of the Victorian brolga, a bird whose cause he championed for much of his professional life. He noted that even the handful of brolgas foraging in the few large, well-vegetated freshwater wetlands still remaining in wildlife reserves were forced to flee during duck-hunting season because of the uproar caused by shooters. Such panicked dispersals severely disrupt the brolga's vital socialising routines.

What was needed, Graham proposed, was the creation of several large, strategically located freshwater refuges with adequate catchments and a buffer zone insulating brolgas from external noise and movement. Research by Birds Australia and others confirms that species once common but now rare or of restricted distribution need large undisturbed areas to thrive.

Adding to the problem of habitat loss, landscape degradation has compromised natural ecosystems and native animals, creating a niche for feral species such as foxes, considered the primary cause of poor brolga breeding success. Indeed, foxes plus a veritable tsunami of other alien animal and plant invaders are the second greatest threat to Australia's biodiversity after land clearing.

John Anderson, the ruddy, robust, instantly likeable owner of the Willaura property where I was camping, has a very low opinion of foxes. 'There's been a fox population explosion,' he announced. 'All the dead foxes on the roads? Never saw 'em when I was a kid.'

Foxes and rabbits were introduced into Australia by landowners wishing to retain pastoral pastimes pursued in England. Victorian gentry with a penchant for riding to hounds initially released foxes in the mid-1800s and they spread rapidly; by the 1930s they had colonised most of the continent except for the wet tropics. Their arrival had a fatal impact on medium-sized native mammals and ground-nesting birds. Not having co-evolved with this sagacious hunter, they are naive in its ways, with few adaptive strategies to avoid predation. Ornithologist Don White reported increased sightings of Victorian brolgas between 1978–1981 that he attributed to a reduction in fox numbers due to increased hunting for the fur trade. Hunting pressure subsequently sagged because of declining pelt prices and increased firearm restrictions and fox numbers rebounded. Current estimates suggest that there's a minimum of 1 million foxes in Victoria, with over four foxes per square kilometre in rural central Victoria and up to 16 foxes per square kilometre in urban areas.

John Anderson and other landholders whose properties support brolgas were outraged by the cessation of the state government's $3 million Enhanced Fox Management bounty program, introduced in June

With the steep, blue, saw-tooth peaks of the Grampians beyond, a flight of brolgas prepares to join grazing black Angus cattle on a harvested cereal crop in western Victoria. The brolgas return early each summer—one day there are none, then out of the blue a high, wild trumpeting announces an advance party that drifts down to settle lightly on the nearest stubble field.

2003, mainly to reduce lamb kills. Despite paying bounty on 150,822 fox tails in the first year, a scientific evaluation found that reductions in the fox population sufficient to keep numbers down for the long term occurred in less than 4 per cent of the state.

Paying a bounty on foxes isn't a panacea; the lack of targeting may even stimulate reproductive rates through the disruption of fox social groups. In the hope of achieving the broad-scale, consistent control required to sustain fox population reductions, the remaining two years of the management program focused on targeted, coordinated baiting in high-priority lambing areas. Perhaps rescue will ultimately arrive via a CSIRO fox control program based on bait-delivered sterilisation that is currently in development.

Compounding the problems of habitat loss and introduced predators, electric wires are known to kill brolgas in our dangerous modern world. Big birds and powerlines form a volatile and destructive mix, particularly for birds that often fly at dawn and dusk, as do brolgas. Not only are birds killed but collisions often lead to costly interruptions to the electricity supply.

In 1985–86, Peter Goldstraw and Philip Du Guesclin undertook a year-long survey to assess bird casualties resulting from collisions with the 500-kilovolt Geelong–Portland transmission line that crosses wetland-rich farmlands and effectively bisects Victoria's main brolga breeding area. The researchers walked a zigzag course along a 6-kilometre transect on four consecutive days every four weeks, scanning for struck birds and found 130 kills—35 per cent of them black swans and 29 per cent straw-necked ibis—belonging to twenty species.

Actual casualties must have been much higher as long grass made finding remains difficult, and foxes, ravens and hawks would have scavenged many. One farmer told the researchers that he routinely removed bird carcasses when sheep were lambing to reduce the presence of foxes among the ewes. Multiply the results of this survey by the thousands of kilometres of powerlines around the country and total bird mortality must be huge.

During random inspections at other sites along the same transmission line, two dead brolgas were found. Like other big birds such as swans,

OPPOSITE: *Shrieking in indignant alarm, a yellow-tailed black cockatoo flares its wings and bright yellow tail band. The long-carrying discordant cries of a flock of these cockatoos flying slowly over the trees is a familiar sound in the pine plantations and eucalypt forests of south-east Australia.*

brolgas are not able to take rapid evasive action. Ideally, Goldstraw and Du Guesclin recommended, powerlines should be underground, but where the expense is prohibitive, they should be as far away as possible from important wetlands, particularly those supporting breeding and flocking sites of species at risk of collision.

Attempts to reverse the southern brolga's century and a half of ill fortune began to take shape in the 1960s at Serendip Wildlife Research Station. The internationally recognised 250-hectare facility at Lara, 60 kilometres south-west of Melbourne, was founded to monitor wild bird populations and as a breeding station for threatened brolgas, Australian bustards and magpie geese. A primary mission was the establishment of a captive flock of brolgas to raise offspring for restoration to the wild.

Bred by artificial insemination but incubated and reared by their parents, 25 of Serendip's brolgas, banded and initially soft released into a fox-proof acclimatisation enclosure for five weeks, were freed at three sites in western Victoria in 1996. Although information on the progress of the released birds was haphazard, there were confirmed sightings of some of them bonding with wild birds. Three of them were attacked and killed by territorial males at the commencement of the breeding season. In all, eight of the released brolgas died, two were recaptured and fifteen were known to have survived. There is still a lot to learn and at the moment no further releases are planned.

In recent years, Serendip's emphases have shifted to public education and managing the property as a Western Plains wildlife sanctuary. Brolgas are still bred here, however, as I discovered on the final leg of my Victorian tour. 'Cranes reared in captivity can be very aggressive,' ranger-in-charge Mike Helman advised as he showed me around Serendip's complex of sturdy pens and spacious compounds. As we walked past, several cranky brolgas stretched their necks in piercing unison calls to warn that this was their territory.

Shortly after joining Serendip, education ranger Suzanne Coates learnt just how hostile these very strong birds can be. While working her first solo weekend, the novice ranger entered a breeding enclosure with food for a nesting couple incubating an egg. The newly protective male uncharacteristically met her as she opened the gate and immediately launched a flapping, claws-first attack. One quick kick of his powerful leg bowled her over and the furious bird followed up with a flurry of painful pecks. Desperately trying to fend off his long hard javelin bill, Suzanne struggled to her feet and made a dash for the enclosure with the male in hot pursuit.

'Once inside I was able to give him the slip and escape, locking the gate behind me. Naturally I was shaken up but I clearly remember thinking as I was being attacked that the brolga's threatened status had nothing to do with their lack of aggression or go.'

For all their understandable distrust of humans, the fate of Victoria's brolgas will be determined in large part by people, in particular the daily actions and long-term aspirations of brolga admirers working under widely varying circumstances. The combination of their coordinated recommendations, basic biological information and updated status reports will hopefully help ensure that these charismatic birds find safe passage through the uncertain times ahead.

Suzanne Coates, education ranger at Serendip Sanctuary, wing-clips a recently fledged young brolga while volunteer Jarrah MacGregor (left), ranger Mike Smith and ranger-in-charge Mike Helman help to restrain it. Several pairs of hands are needed to subdue this very strong bird.

CHAPTER NINE

Bool Lagoon

This place, the sacred lake, was known as the great ceremonial ground, the meeting place for birds that are called by the names of the old tribes—the black swans, the pelicans and the ducks. Blue-tongued lizards glide through the grass and the bittern calls 'oom, oom, oom'.

—ABORIGINAL CREATION STORY, *AUSTRALIAN DREAMING*¹

Spring in Bool Lagoon. Generous winter rainfall has ensured a time of plenty. Amid the warmth and harmony and bountiful water as clear as a grebe's eye come whispers of an age of paradise.

As I watch, the lagoon's birdlife sets the day in motion. Moment by moment, a lustrous dawn reveals a great hive of life wheeling around a grove of swamp paperbarks growing in the main basin. Birds that had spent the dark hours with chicks in their rookeries are hurrying forth to forage for food.

The blur of wings, the ancient cries, the sheer primal urgency of the myriad waterfowl is like an image of Earth's first morning. The sky is aswirl with arrowhead formations of ibises, the iridescent shot-silk plumage of an occasional glossy ibis reflecting the early light. Long strings of cormorants wing across the wetlands, moving smoothly as projectiles. The sharp white outlines of egrets and spoonbills flap by; I can see their wing joints working under their feathers. In a magical coherence of motion, a huge flock of whiskered terns banks over the shoreline, seeming to move in obedience to one mind. Swans, with their charcoal-black wet sheen, red bill and thin angularity, anchor the calm waters, their necks looping from the surface like sinuous arms. Black-winged stilts, yapping like puppies, stalk gingerly through the shallows on spindly red legs, selecting food with jabs and probes of their long darning needle of a bill. Ducks bobbing far offshore leave a drifting wake. There are marsh harriers, too. Even an Australian hobby, a handsome and dashing falcon that specialises in capturing small birds in mid-air but now sits atop a fence post, looking as emblematic as an heraldic symbol. A land of water full of life! All intensified by the beauty of the setting.

At this time of year intercontinental waders stop by in their thousands to refuel. Sharp-tailed sandpipers, greenshanks and red-necked stints skitter across pond edges like wind gusts, perforating the mud in their search for tiny insects. Nineteen species of migrant shorebirds have been recorded here, including rare sightings such as the long-toed stint, pectoral sandpiper and a single record of a little ringed plover, only the second for Australia.

PAGES 148–9: *A moody blue twilight envelops Bool Lagoon; knowing a landscape's sounds and silences, how it feels and smells, sets it forever in its own special light.*

OPPOSITE: *The air rustles with the passage of fast-flying grey teal rising from Round Swamp. As the favoured prey of hunters, teal are shy and flighty in Bool Lagoon, which has a long history of duck shooting.*

These fidgety birds of passage are the common property and responsibility of many nations, and in Australia they are afforded special protection under agreements with China and Japan.

Bool's five interconnecting basins plus Little Bool Lagoon form a mosaic of dense reeds and rushes interspersed with open water that shelters 79 waterbird species, of which 67 are resident or regular visitors and 49 breed here, 29 of them regularly. It provides sanctuary for threatened species such as the musk duck, Australasian shoveler, Lewin's rail, Latham's and painted snipe, and Baillon's crake. It is the only place in south-east South Australia where the little bittern, magpie goose and plumed whistling duck have been recorded. Its importance as a summer refuge for the up to 50,000 ducks it commonly supports is emphasised when one of the world's rarest waterfowl, the freckled duck, arrives here in the hundreds after the northern wetlands dry up. Black swan numbers vary between 1000–5000, and this lush haven frequently hosts more than 1 per cent of Australia's total population of great egrets and Australasian shovelers.

This freshwater wetland complex is also the brolga's last great flocking site in South Australia. But important as that role now is, it wasn't the plight of the southern brolga that prompted the push to have Bool Lagoon preserved for bird conservation. Rather, it was the threat posed to the traditional breeding grounds of thousands of ibises that rallied local farmers in protest against a plan to drain this critical waterfowl refuge.

When conditions are favourable, with water levels high enough to surround their nest sites, colonies of more than 50,000 ibises gather to breed at Bool's semi-permanent lagoons. Equipped with a long, downward-curved bill designed to probe for insects, straw-necked ibises in particular were quick to take advantage of the cornucopia of cockchafer beetles, crickets, grass-hoppers, cutworms and various larvae attracted to the ploughed paddocks of cereal crops and lucerne that had replaced the native heaths and grasslands.

An ibis can eat up to 25 per cent of its own body weight in pasture pests each day. Over 2000 grass-hoppers were found in the stomach of one straw-necked ibis and it's been estimated that a flock of 5000 can consume as much as 1 tonne of invertebrates daily, with over 70 per cent comprising insects that have some economic importance on the farm.

Farmers may not have been aware of the statistics in the early 1960s when they voted to rescue Bool Lagoon, but they knew enough to recognise the symbiotic relationship that existed between the pasture pests and the bird they referred to as 'the farmer's friend'. Their decision resulted in the salvation of one of the largest and most diverse marshes in southern Australia, part of the mere 11 per cent of south-east South Australia's former wetlands that remain today. But it very nearly didn't happen.

Squatters began settling these fertile limestone plains midway between Melbourne and Adelaide from the early 1840s, but the lure of well-watered pastures also presented them with one of their most intractable problems. In the wake of reliable winter rainfall

Perching on a favourite fence post while watching for prey, an Australian hobby also keeps a wary eye on a human intruder. This dashing little falcon sometimes courses open farmlands like a huge delicate swallow as it pursues dragonflies, but in its role as fierce raptor it captures birds up to its own size in midair chases or in power dives from above.

When the rain gods are kind, Bool Lagoon is one of South Australia's richest wetlands. Its nutrient-rich waters attract a fascinating profusion of wild creatures, from teeming invertebrates to more than 150 bird species.

averaging 600 millimetres annually, water run-off from the 1215-square-kilometre catchment flowed along ill-defined high-volume creeks with headwaters in western Victoria and descended onto the low-lying Naracoorte Plain, seasonally flooding huge areas of land.

Native animals have evolved to capitalise on high-water events and respond with an explosion of new life. But the Anglo-Celts who settled the Mosquito Plains to the north of Bool Lagoon understandably regarded the waterlogging of the wide blacksoil plains for six months of the year as an impediment to good farming. To safeguard permanent homes and roads and bring more land into crop production, it was essential to make the floodwaters' flow more predictable, to replace primitive forces with a domesticated regime. The landscape would have to be reshaped into a European ideal.

In 1958 the South Eastern Drainage Board proposed draining Bool Lagoon by building a deep gullet (or outlet drain) across its bed. The idea was to divert Mosquito Creek's flow away from the Mosquito Plains farmlands and, via the outlet drain, into the ocean at Beachport. It seemed an all too familiar scenario: farming and development, while on the other side, birds—and the fragile dream of retaining their natural habitat.

Thankfully, farmers' concerns regarding the effect draining Bool Lagoon might have on groundwater levels, as well as on the ibises, and by duck shooters faced with the prospect of losing their quarry, saw the usual no-holds-barred development replaced by a sensible compromise. Bool Lagoon would serve the dual role of waterbird habitat and ponding basin (or sump) for the whole district's floodwaters. Water storage was achieved by enlarging Mosquito Creek into an inlet channel and heavy flows are released at a controlled rate through regulator gates. At maximum capacity, Bool Lagoon's system fills with water to cover 2530 hectares.

In 1967, the 3023-hectare Bool Lagoon Game Reserve and the contiguous 198-hectare Hacks Lagoon Conservation Park were gazetted, and in 1985 both were included on the List of Wetlands of International Importance under the Ramsar Convention.

Secure in its sturdy stick-nest built into the low branches of a swamp paperbark in Bool's main basin, this late-hatching glossy ibis chick is part of a bustling breeding colony of straw-necked and white ibises as well as other members of its own species.

This south-east corner of South Australia has changed dramatically since a nineteenth-century settler described it as resembling 'a nobleman's park on a large scale'. The changes are reflected in the name Bool, a Boandik word meaning 'sweet drink', a reference to the nectar sipped from the blossoms of the once profuse banksias that have long since given way to wheat, barley, safflower, linseed, potatoes, hay crops and improved pastures for cattle and sheep. Thanks to family farms, the region is prosperous, and though Bool's wetlands are now artificially manipulated, they retain a great and venerable beauty and the birds keep coming, perpetuating its importance as a breeding site and dry season refuge.

There is a seamlessness to this natural world, the way energy flows from sun to plants and water, to insects, fish, birds and mammals. But such connectedness can easily be disrupted. For all its apparent durability and resistance, this is a delicate system, establishing itself with difficulty, growing slowly and uncertain to rebound if disturbed. Proclaiming a park or reserve is only the first step. Establishing protected areas involves setting up management plans to ensure the protection of fragments of what used to be a continuous system. Which sounds deceptively easy but given nature's complex and sensitive balances, never is.

Just how precarious those balances can be is evidenced by the fate of the focal point of Bool's ecosystem, the dense 40-hectare woodland of swamp paperbarks (*Melaleuca halmaturorum*) that serves as a nesting rookery for ibises, egrets, spoonbills and

Seen from a distance, the glossy ibis looks dull black but, close-up, sunlight reveals that its plumage is really an exquisitely rich purple-brown with a metallic iridescent-green sheen on the wings; its face is blue-green and its bill greenish brown. The smallest of Australia's three ibis species, the glossy ibis wanders nomadically in search of feeding grounds.

cormorants. The shaggy-barked trees are a relic of the natural water regime that existed before flood control measures were installed and are a fine example of the near impossibility of interfering with a natural wetland ecosystem at any point without causing repercussions elsewhere.

The difference between Bool's wet and dry seasons can be striking. One is full of energy, in a landscape of brimming marshes; the other is brown and austere. In the past, the lagoons grew or shrank according to a dynamic cycle that balanced the amount of winter precipitation plus rain run-off against the level of evaporation during the boiling-point summers. Seasons

greatly influence water levels but, under present management arrangements, they can be expected to vary from waist deep after winter to completely dry every second year during the summer and autumn months.

While paperbarks can tolerate many years of continual flooding, they need at least three years of dry conditions for their seeds to germinate and for the slow-growing seedlings to reach about 1 metre in height, by which time they can survive flood conditions. With Bool Lagoon required to handle the total floodwaters for the district, prolonged high water levels have prevented new seedlings from establishing. The original trees have

Large flocks of brolgas, like this one at Bool's Black Rush Swamp, can only occur where food is abundant. In Bool Lagoon's large, open sedge marshes, brolgas are able to dig for their more traditional fare of tubers while in the harvested wheat fields that border the wetlands they can feed on an abundance of gleanings.

A slender, 42-millimetre-long brown tree frog, Litoria ewingi, *clings to an acacia branch encrusted with colourful lichens. Despite its name, in Bool Lagoon the brown tree frog is pale green with brown markings. It is one of Bool's eleven species of amphibians.*

passed from maturity into senescence and one by one are dying of old age. In the last 50 years there has been a 40 per cent reduction in the paperbarks' canopy cover. New stands of paperbarks have been planted along the more recent high-water mark and are used by a small number of nesting birds. It's feared, however, that most colonial breeders, who require their nesting grounds to be completely surrounded by water usually at least a metre deep, will reject them as too exposed.

The drive to harness the region's floodwaters, while at the same time trying to maintain nature in an artificially protected enclave, has had side effects that were often unpredictable and which have taken decades to become fully apparent. These bird-haunted marshlands were thousands of years in the making.

They are the ecological equivalent of estuaries, and just as important in the life cycle of many bird species as estuaries are to fish and crustaceans.

It's a complex system and anybody who wants to understand it eventually finds their way to Jack Bourne. This easygoing, personable man of 60 or so grew up on a property adjoining Bool, to a family that goes back three generations in these parts. His lifelong fascination and involvement with the area's wildlife has made his reputation as a naturalist, so when early in the new year he sent a message that read, 'Counted 129 brolgas last weekend. Looks great!' I didn't hesitate.

I returned to Bool Lagoon in summer, when the sun rises early and hot. At this time of year the marshes ring with eerie music—brolga bugling. Their distinctive calls symbolise, I think, the spirit of the place. Just as wetlands are among South Australia's most threatened ecosystems, so brolgas—reported as 'very common' from the Adelaide Plains to Yorke Peninsula and the Lower North before the late 1800s—have been reduced to rare in the south-east and far north-east, and vagrant everywhere else in the state.

The decline of brolga populations in southern Australia has been attributed mainly to the widespread draining of wetlands, but in south-eastern South Australia, although draining began in the late 1860s, it wasn't until the 1940s that work started on the extensive system of drains that exists today. Nor would drainage have led to such a sudden crash in the number of adult birds. Brolga authority Gavin Blackman attributes their dramatic decline to the catastrophic droughts of 1880–1920 plus the impact of agriculture on traditional post-breeding flocking sites and the harassment of the birds as agricultural pests. The last, direct human persecution, almost certainly played a big role and by the early 1900s they were already 'getting rare'.

The relationship between brolgas and settler farmers was the precise opposite of that enjoyed by the ibis. Farmers complained that native companions were most persistent in their attack on the crops. Brolgas were in the way—a pest species that had to be taken care of. As one old-timer, Jack McArthur, recalled: 'My grandfather came from Mount Gambier to Millicent [west of Bool] in 1872, after the flats had been drained. He told me that brolgas were a problem with cereal crops when sown by hand and harrowed in. They had to sow poisoned grain to get any sort of crop.'

The unsuspecting birds scratched in the dirt with their long bills, disinterred the poisoned grain, ate it and died in their thousands. No questions were asked; men acted out of necessity. There was precious little sentimentalism involved in the struggle to make farming pay on the Australian frontier.

'Freshly sown crops were the problem. Once they had germinated they were okay,' Jack Bourne told me at Bourne's Bird Museum, a delightfully handmade tourist attraction he runs with his charming wife, Pat, on their farm, 10 kilometres west of Bool Lagoon. 'Back in the early '50s my dad used to send me out with a .22 to guard the oats. I never shot a brolga but I would've if I could've.'

The brolgas' fear of humans has never gone away. As I drove from my campsite on Gunawar Peninsula

At Hacks Lagoon, a magpie goose stretches its wings. An ultimately successful program to reintroduce magpie geese to the park was almost derailed when several hundred died from lead poisoning after ingesting spent shot pellets they picked up from the marsh bottom while feeding.

overlooking Hacks Lagoon's dense reedbeds, a small flock of brolgas foraging fallen grain in neighbouring stubblefields took flight at the mere sound of my approaching vehicle, long before they saw me. They glided to the far side of Black Rush Swamp's broad sedge meadows where they obviously felt less at risk. Yet even then my presence unsettled them and they kept a wary eye on me until I departed.

In the last half-century, the loss of suitable habitat has reduced south-east South Australia's brolga breeding population to a mere ten to twenty pairs. Those I had come to see are mostly visitors from nearby breeding grounds in western Victoria. Each year around 100–150 post-breeding brolgas congregate at Bool Lagoon between January and May, while the south-east's total flocking population varies yearly between 150–250 birds depending on conditions, a figure that has remained relatively static in recent times.

A contemporary management controversy that impacts brolgas, at least indirectly, is the vexed question of Bool's status as a duck-hunting venue. Its proclamation as a game reserve means that Bool functions both to preserve wildlife while at the same time permitting a controlled harvest of ducks, mainly grey teal and Pacific black ducks. Private shoots have been held here since the early 1920s, when 'the colossal number of ducks would rise almost like thunder and darken the sky'. The first public shoot in 1969 hosted 300 hunters and in subsequent years there have been up to 2000 shooters.

Bool Lagoon's statutes allow a maximum of six hunting days each year although the timing of the open season, bag limits and permitted species may vary depending on seasonal conditions and population trends. It's a practice that has attracted increasing controversy, with each hunt attended by protest groups of animal liberationists who mount wounded-duck rescue operations. In 1980 the shooting of between 500–1000 freckled ducks seeking drought refuge at Bool stirred up a hornet's nest of complaints.

'There's also the disturbance factor,' Jack Bourne pointed out. 'At the first shot the brolgas flee and they really don't have too many other places to go.' The argument for and against the shoot at Bool has raged in the local press and beyond, although since 1997 there's been a moratorium on hunting pending the outcome of a new management plan. I asked Jack his opinion. 'I'm not against duck hunting in principle,' he told me. 'Heaven knows, I've shot enough ducks in my time.' He paused. 'But it's not right for Bool. I'd be really disappointed if its status isn't changed from game reserve to conservation park.'

A sinister by-product of the duck shoots nearly derailed one of Bool's most successful conservation initiatives—the reintroduction of magpie geese. These noisy, boldly marked birds formerly bred as far south as Bool Lagoon, but a combination of habitat destruction, hunting and poisoning when they grazed grain crops had brought about their disappearance from

OPPOSITE: *Pied cormorants gather to preen in an ancient swamp paperbark. When it floods and the surrounding water forms a barrier, this paperbark woodland near the eastern side of the main Bool Lagoon basin supports a breeding rookery of several hundred thousand ibises, cormorants, egrets, herons and spoonbills. At such times, Bool is the image of a world in harmony with nature and a place of the soul.*

South Australia by 1911. Then more than half a century later a project was initiated to re-establish a free-flying population, but a hidden danger would threaten their return.

In 1968, eighteen adult magpie geese from the Northern Territory were pinioned and released into an enclosure at Hacks Lagoon, with follow-up releases involving goslings mostly obtained from artificially incubated eggs. There were false starts and setbacks but by 1985 slow progress had been made, with some 320 geese thriving and breeding at Hacks Lagoon. Then disaster struck.

In 1986, resident ranger Mike Harper began finding dead and dying geese. A count showed that the population had crashed to 180. Post-mortem examinations at a veterinary laboratory revealed lead shotgun pellets in the birds' gizzards. Many waterbirds swallow grit, scooped up on or just below the beds of lakes and lagoons to help them grind up their food. When they ingest lead it poisons them, often resulting in death by starvation.

Birds known to be in danger of leadshot poisoning include ducks, geese, coots and swans. Mike Harper also discovered 50 dead swans. The die-off resulted in more bad press for the hunting lobby. The following year regulations were drafted outlawing leadshot and now only non-toxic steel, bismuth or molybdenum shot is legal.

During my first visit in spring, the falsetto honking of magpie geese overflying my campsite began at daybreak and didn't cease until after dusk. Now, in summer, during the laying season, they had become secretive and silent to safeguard the whereabouts of eggs and chicks. It was a very good sign. Encouraging breeding results have seen their numbers increase to a present population of around 500, a healthy nucleus from which to launch a magpie goose comeback to southern Australia.

On my farewell tour of Bool Lagoon Game Reserve I was pleased to see five Cape Barren geese, the remnants of an another, less successful reintroduction. They watched my arrival at Round Swamp against a backdrop of grey teal rising in great crying flocks. Unique to Australia, this plump, ash-grey, stumpy-billed goose was almost hunted to extinction by the early 1900s. Now one of the rarest waterfowl in the world, they nest on islands off the south coast and fly between the islands and the mainland during the non-breeding season.

The gravel road I was driving on through this north-western sector of the park had deteriorated into a rutted track that twisted and dipped over crescent-shaped ridges called lunettes, formed over aeons by sedimentary deposits blown from the lagoon floor during dry periods. A pair of blue-winged parrots eating thistle seeds on the side of the track got up ahead of me, their wings opening and closing like fans lined with deep royal blue.

I passed a mob of pink and grey galahs waddling slowly along in a closely spaced crowd, selecting fallen grain in harvested wheatfields that extend into the reserve. Once thought of as exclusively a resident of the arid interior, this opportunistic cockatoo's spectacular spread over the last century into more populated regions has been attributed to forest felling that created grasslands and paddocks of cereal crops where seed-eaters like

Among the more than 10,000 ducks that Bool Lagoon regularly supports is an irregular visitor that arrives in numbers ranging from a few individuals to hundreds when its northern habitat dries out. It is the freckled duck—one of the rarest waterfowl in the world. The survival of this unusual swan-like duck depends on expansive shallow swamps with dense vegetation as breeding grounds and on drought refuges that have permanent water.

galahs thrive. Travelling along corridors of cleared land, they fanned out from one region to the next, assisted by a proliferation of farm dams. In Bool they went from being unknown before the 1930s to becoming one of its commonest birds.

By the time I got back to camp it was late afternoon. The weight of the sun had begun to lift, so I set out for a stroll along Gunawar Walk on a path that leads across a boardwalk and onto Hacks Island. A green filigree of tall backlit phragmites and their sharp twilight reflections contrasted sharply with the silver water. Startled ibises and spoonbills exploded into flight with wingbeats that sounded like billowing sails. These secluded backwater reed thickets are used as nest sites by some sacred and straw-necked ibises. They build a platform of sticks on a flattened bed of reeds when there isn't enough tree space to go around.

This is true swamp, to use the old derogatory name, although it never had an evil connotation among naturalists. Its peaty water, warm and shallow, is thick with nutrients and teems with whirligig beetles, backswimmers, water boatmen, water measurers, mayfly nymphs and mosquito pupae. Fish are feeding on this smorgasbord of protein. Choruses of frogs and cicadas belch and drone.

It's a good place to just sit and wait as the shadows lengthen. The sweetest part is waiting; it produces a transcendent, settling clarity. For quite a long time nothing new happens, then an eastern snake-necked freshwater turtle rises to the surface, gulps air and slowly sinks again. I am being watched, I know, from all around, and from the branches up above, by many different eyes. It's just a matter of staying still until the wild creatures are reassured that I'm not a threat. A copperhead snake appears, swimming between floating fronds of duckweed and milfoil, its body forming and re-forming itself like an S-shaped spring. A bright red dragonfly hovers beside me, eyes bulbous, its body bending to form a horseshoe. It drops and jabs the tip of its abdomen like a syringe through the water's taut skin, perhaps laying eggs. From out of the gathering gloom comes the deep, bodeful boom of a male Australasian bittern.

The evening is warm, clear and windless. Above the horizon, the sky reddens as the sun sinks towards a steel-blue cloud stained with crimson. The approach of night has activated clouds of midges that swirl above the lagoon's pink- and gold-tinted surface like pointillist patches of ground fog. Mixed hunting parties of tree martins and welcome swallows dart and wheel into the swarm.

The image of Bool Lagoon that I shall carry longest in my memory is of sunset skies etched with strings of homing ibises. Of a pair of brolgas silhouetted against the thick mauve light, the majestic creatures returning to their roost in measured flight, long necks outstretched and long legs trailing behind their tails. The golden bugles of their voices drifted resonant and clear across the marsh, a poignant exchange that carried with it, so I imagined, a note of hope little heard since man first lifted a gun or an axe and took far more than he needed.

As the sun dips, a cloud extinguishes the sunset, tinting Bool Lagoon's surface with shades of blue and grey. A late-feeding black swan silently selects aquatic plants; the only sound is the chirring of superb fairy-wrens and thornbills foraging among the paperbarks. At times like these, Bool Lagoon feels like an earthly paradise.

Notes

CHAPTER 1

1. Collected by Alice Moyle in eastern Arnhem Land in 1963 and used by permission. Kurruwurwur is the Nunggubuyu peoples' onomatopoeic name for the brolga and wonderfully evokes the bird's low, rolling plaintive voice. Karangarri is the brolgas' mythical ancestral home. This song is sung and danced by men, accompanied by the didjeridu. Women and girls watched but did not take part. Dancers performed solo, in pairs and more often as a group. Fifteen or more men would follow one another in circular formation or advancing, side by side, in a line with bird-like hops and arms outstretched as wings. The chirping sounds made by the dancers intermingled with the bird-like refrains of the singers.

2. Named after the Iranian town where, in 1971, an intergovernmental convention was dedicated to the conservation and 'wise use' of wetlands. As of December 2000 there were 123 contracting countries with 1044 wetland sites totalling 78.5 million hectares. Australia has 56 Ramsar sites covering approximately 5.3 million hectares.

CHAPTER 3

1. Although the name Great Dividing Range is widely used, it is misleading. In reality it is not a continuous mountain range.

2. Fourteen recognised subspecies of cranes survive.

3. A billabong is formed when a section of a river becomes isolated from the main channel as it alters course over low, flat country. Only during floods is the billabong rejoined to the parent river.

CHAPTER 4

1. Fire regimes are the sequence of fires typical of a given area. There are four key components: fire intensity, fire type (for example, crown or ground fire), frequency and season.

2. Tropical Savannas CRC, *Cape York—Fire*, <savanna.cdu.edu.au/information/cy/cy_fr.html>.

CHAPTER 5

1. G. Barrett, A. Silcocks, S. Barry, R. Cunningham and R. Poulter, *The New Atlas of Australian Birds*, Royal Australasian Ornithologists Union, Hawthorn East, Victoria, 2003.

2. Geographic Information Systems—a combination of elements designed to store, retrieve, manipulate and display geographic data.

CHAPTER 7

1. The Murray River and its largest tributary, the Darling, form a catchment known as the Murray–Darling Basin that drains one-seventh of the continent. Annually it produces 40 per cent of Australia's agriculture (worth $8.5 billion), including 90 per cent of its irrigated agriculture (worth $3 billion) and manufacturing worth $11 billion, 70 per cent of which is dependent on agriculture.

2. The amount of 750 gigalitres (gL) is about one-quarter of the capacity of the Hume Dam or one and a half times the volume of Sydney Harbour.

3. John Gould, *The Birds of Australia*, 7 vols, 36 parts, 600 plates, London, 1840–48.

4. Threatened means that a species is vulnerable or endangered and may become extinct.

5. Adapted from Murray J. McIntyre, *Conservation of the Brolga* Grus rubicundus *in Victoria: The role of private land*, Dept of Conservation and Natural Resources, Ballarat, 1995, Figure 2.2. Used by permission.

CHAPTER 8

1. P.L. Brown (ed.), 'Memoirs recorded at Geelong, Victoria, by Captain Foster Fyans (1790–1870)'. Transcribed from his holograph manuscript and given by his descendents to the State Library, Melbourne, 1962.

2. Wilhelm Habel, quoted in Rod Bird, *The Hamilton Region of South-western Victoria: An historical perspective of landscape, settlement and impacts on Aborigine occupants, flora and fauna*, Dept of Primary Industries, Hamilton, Victoria, 2004.

3. G.T. Lloyd quoted in D.N. Conley and C. Dennis (eds), *The Western Plains: A natural and social history*, Australian Institute of Agricultural Science, Victoria, 1983.

CHAPTER 9

1. Abridged from Jennifer Isaacs (ed.), *Australian Dreaming: 40,000 years of Aboriginal history*, Lansdowne Press, Sydney, 1980.

Bibliography

Archibald, George W. and Lewis, James C., *Cranes: Their biology, husbandry and conservation*, US Dept of the Interior, National Biological Service, Washington DC, and International Crane Foundation, Baraboo, Wisconsin, 1996.

Archibald, George W. and Swengel, Scott R., *Comparative Ecology and Behaviour of Eastern Sarus Cranes and Brolgas in Australia*, International Crane Foundation, Baraboo, Wisconsin, 1985.

Arnol, J.D., White, D.M. and Hastings, I., *Management of the Brolga in Victoria*, Dept of Conservation, Lands, Fisheries and Wildlife Service, Melbourne, 1984.

The Australian Wildlife Year, Reader's Digest (Australia), Sydney, 1989.

Badman, F.J., *Birds and the Boredrains of Inland South Australia*, Nature Conservation Society of South Australia, Adelaide, 1987.

Badman, F.J., Arnold, B.K. and Bell, S.L., *A Natural History of the Lake Eyre Region: A visitor's guide*, The South Australian National Parks and Wildlife Service, Port Augusta, 1981.

Barrett, G., Silcocks, A., Barry, S., Cunningham, R. and Poulter, R., *The New Atlas of Australian Birds*, Royal Australasian Ornithologists Union, Hawthorn East, Victoria, 2003.

Bird, Rod, *The Original Nature of South-western Victoria*, Wetland Forum, Glenelg Hopkins CMA and Wetland Care Australia, 2000.

——, *The Hamilton Region of South-western Victoria: An historical perspective of landscape, settlement and impacts on Aborigine occupants, flora and fauna*, Dept of Primary Industries, Hamilton, Victoria, 2004.

Blackman, J.G., Aerial Survey Methods for Population and Ecological Studies of the Brolga, unpublished Master of Science thesis, University of Queensland, Brisbane, 1977.

——, *A Directory of Important Wetlands in Australia*, Dept of the Environment and Heritage, Canberra, and Queensland Environmental Protection Agency, Brisbane, 2001.

Bransbury, John, *The Brolga in South-eastern South Australia: A report on a study conducted during 1989–1990*, South Australian Dept of Environment and Planning, Adelaide, 1991.

Brown, P.L. (ed.), 'Memoirs recorded at Geelong, Victoria, by Captain Foster Fyans (1790–1870)', transcribed from his holograph manuscript and given by his descendants to the State Library, Melbourne, 1962.

Conley, D.N. and Dennis, C. (eds), *The Western Plains: A natural and social history*, Australian Institute of Agricultural Science, Victoria, 1983.

Douglas, Michael and Bunn, Stuart, *Weed Management and the Bio-diversity and Ecological Processes of Tropical Wetlands*, Dept of the Environment and Heritage, Canberra, and Centre for Tropical Wetlands Management, Darwin, 2004.

Encyclopedia of Australian Wildlife, Reader's Digest (Australia), Sydney, 1997.

Frith, Dawn and Frith, Clifford, *Cape York Peninsula: A natural history*, Bloomings Books, Sydney, 2006.

Frith, H.J. (ed.), *Birds in the Australian High Country*, Angus & Robertson, Sydney, 1976.

Fullerton, Ticky, *Watershed: Deciding our water future*, ABC Books, Melbourne, 2001.

Garnett, Stephen, *Economics of Lure Cropping to Reduce Crop Damage by Cockatoos*, Environmental Protection Agency, Cairns, 2004.

Garnett, Stephen and Crowley, G.M., *The Action Plan for Australian Birds*, Environment Australia, Canberra, 2000.

Gill, Malcolm, Woinarski, J.C.Z. and York, Allan, *Australia's Biodiversity—Responses to Fire: Plants, birds and invertebrates*, Dept of Environment and Heritage, Canberra, 1999.

Goldstraw, Peter W. and Du Guesclin, Philip B., *Bird Casualties from Collisions with a 500 KV Transmission Line in Southwestern Victoria, Australia*, Dept of Conservation, Forests and Lands, Victoria, 1991.

Gould, John, *The Birds of Australia*, 7 vols, 36 parts, 600 plates, London, 1840–48.

Grant, John, 'Secrets of the sarus crane', *Wingspan*, vol. 14, no. 4, 2004.

Harding, Claire, Use of Remote Sensing and Geographic Information Systems to Predict Suitable Breeding Habitat for the Brolga in South-western Victoria, unpublished Honours thesis, University of Ballarat, 2001.

Harper, M.J., 'Waterbird dynamics at Bool Lagoon, South Australia, 1983–87', *Australian Wildlife Research*, vol. 17, no. 2, 1990.

——, 'The re-establishment of magpie geese at Bool Lagoon, South Australia', *South Australian Ornithologist*, vol. 31, 1990.

Harper M.J. and Hindmarsh, M., 'Lead poisoning in magpie geese *Anseranas semipalmata* from ingested lead pellet at Bool Lagoon Game Reserve (South Australia)', *Australian Wildlife Research*, vol. 17, no. 2, 1990.

Harris, James, 'Cranes, people and nature: Preserving the balance', spoken submission to The Future of Cranes and Wetlands symposium, International Crane Foundation, Baraboo, Wisconsin, 1994.

Harris, J. and Langenberg, J., 'Cranes in a crowded world', *ICF Bugle*, vol. 22, no. 2, Baraboo, Wisconsin, 1996.

Herring, Matthew, The Brolga (*Grus rubicunda*) in the New South Wales and Victorian Riverina: Distribution, breeding habitat and potential role as an umbrella species, unpublished Honours thesis, Charles Sturt University, Albury, 2001.

——, 'Dancing brolgas', *Wingspan*, vol. 14, no. 4, 2004.

Hill, Richard, *A Database of Brolga* (Grus rubicundus) *Nest Sites in Victoria*, Royal Australasian Ornithologists Union, Melbourne, 1992.

Hudson, Dave, *Townsville Town Common 'Common Interest' Project: Revive our wetlands*, Dept of the Environment and Heritage, Canberra, 2004.

Isaacs, Jennifer (ed.), *Australian Dreaming: 40,000 years of Aboriginal history*, Lansdowne Press, Sydney, 1980.

Kingsford, Richard, *Aerial Survey of Waterbirds in Eastern Australia*, Wetland Care Australia, 2001.

Koh, T.S. and Harper, M.J., 'Lead poisoning in black swans, *Cygnus atratus*, exposed to spent lead shot at Bool Lagoon Game Reserve, South Australia', *Australian Wildlife Research*, vol. 15, no. 4, 1988.

Lavery, Hugh (ed.), *Exploration North: Australia's wildlife from desert to reef*, Richmond Hill Press, Melbourne, 1978.

Lawson, Henry, *A Camp-Fire Yarn: Henry Lawson, complete works 1885–1900*, Lansdowne Press, Sydney, 1984.

Low, Tim, *Feral Future*, Viking/Penguin Books Australia, Ringwood, Victoria, 1999.

——, *The New Nature*, Viking/Penguin Books Australia, Ringwood, Victoria, 2002.

McIntyre, Murray J., *Conservation of the Brolga* Grus rubicundus *in Victoria: The role of private land*, Dept of Conservation and Natural Resources, Ballarat, 1995.

Matthiessen, Peter, *The Birds of Heaven: Travels with cranes*, North Point Press, New York, 2001.

Meine, Curt D. and Archibald, George W., *The Cranes: Status survey and conservation action plan*, IUCN, Switzerland, and SSC Crane Specialist Group, USA, 1996.

Milewski, Antoni V., 'A new niche for old Australians? Is Australia ready to support flamingos—again?', *Wingspan*, vol. 14, no. 4, 2004.

Moon, Ron and Moon, Viv, *Cape York: An adventurer's guide*, Kakirra Adventure Press, Victoria, 2001.

Moyle, Alice (compiler), *Songs from the Northern Territory 2: Music from Eastern Arnhem Land*, CD, Australian Institute of Aboriginal and Torres Strait Islander Studies, 1963 (released 1997).

Murdoch, Judy, *Bool Lagoon: A changing balance*, Millicent Print, South Australia, 1991.

Myers, Andrea, Factors Influencing the Nesting Success of Brolgas *Grus rubicundus* in Western Victoria, unpublished Honours thesis, Deakin University, Warrnambool, 2001.

Nicholson, Nan and Nicholson, Hugh, *Australian Rainforest Plants*, Terania Rainforest Publishing, New South Wales, 2000.

Pizzey, Graham, 'Thoroughly modern brolgas', *The Bird Observer*, no. 738, 1994.

——, 'Graham Pizzey's diary notes on brolga flocking sites in south-western Victoria, November 2000–May 2001', unpublished report for the Bird Observers Club of Australia, 2001.

Read, John and Niejalke, Darren, 'Brolgas: The storks of the mound springs', *Xanthopus* (Nature Conservation Society of South Australia newsletter), vol. 13, no. 8, 1995.

Read, John L., *Red Sand Green Heart*, Lothian Books, Melbourne, 2003.

Reader's Digest Complete Book of Australian Birds, Reader's Digest (Australia), Sydney, 1993.

Reardon, Mitch, *The Australian Geographic Book of Corner Country*, Australian Geographic, Sydney, 1995.

Robley, Alan and Wright, John, *Adaptive Experimental Management of Foxes*, annual report for Parks Victoria Technical Series, 2003.

Roth, W.E., *The Queensland Aborigines*, Hesperian Press (facsimile), 1984 reprint of 1897–1910 edition.

Scambler, Elinor, 'Calculating cranes: The first 8 years of a long-term community study in North Queensland', spoken submission for Birds Australia—Northern Queensland Group, Cairns, 2005.

Sheldon, Rebecca, Characterisation and Modelling of Brolga (*Grus rubicundus*) Flocking Habitat in South-Western Victoria, unpublished Honours thesis, University of Ballarat, 2004.

Sinclair, Paul, *The Murray: A river and its people*, Melbourne University Press, 2001.

South Australia Dept of Environment and Planning, *Bool Lagoon Game Reserve and Hacks Lagoon Conservation Park Amended Management Plan*, National Parks and Wildlife Service, 1992.

Stoneman, Mark, *The Cromarty Wetlands*, Wetlands and Grasslands Foundation, Queensland, 1999.

——, 'Practical challenges for wetland managers', spoken submission to the Wetland Care Australia Forum, Townsville, 2003.

Swaby, Ray J., 'Tape-recording sarus cranes', *The Bird Observer*, no. 622, 1983.

Topsell, Edward, *The Fowles of Heaven, or History of Birds conteyning their true and lively figures with the whole description of theire natures*, London, 1614.

Tropical Savannas CRC, 'Cape York—Ferals', *Savanna Explorer*, <savanna.cdu.edu.au/information/cy/cy_fl.html>.

Tropical Savannas CRC, 'Cape York—Fire', *Savanna Explorer*, <savanna.cdu.edu.au/information/cy/cy_fr.html>.

Tropical Savannas CRC, 'Birds of the savannas', *Tropical Topics: An interpretive newsletter*, Queensland Parks and Wildlife Service, 2002.

Vandenbeld, John, *Nature of Australia*, Collins Australia and ABC Enterprises, Sydney, 1988.

Wahliquist, Asa, 'Murray cod disappear from degraded river', *The Weekend Australian*, 16–17 August 1997.

White, D.M., *The Status and Distribution of the Brolga in Victoria, Australia*, Dept of Conservation, Fisheries and Wildlife, Melbourne, 1987.

Young, W.J. (ed.), *Rivers as Ecological Systems: The Murray–Darling Basin*, CSIRO Division of Water and Land Resources, 2001.

Index